YEAST FERMENTATION HANDBOOK

YEAST FERMENTATION HANDBOOK

Essential Guide and Recipes for Beer and Bread Makers

Harmony Sage

ROCKRIDGE
PRESS

Interior and Cover Designer: Jami Spittler
Art Producer: Sue Smith
Editor: Lauren Ladoceour
Production Editor: Ashley Polikoff
Illustrations: © 2019 Clark William Miller; © Shutterstock (pattern).

ISBN: Print 978-1-64152-674-6 | eBook 978-1-64152-675-3

CONTENTS

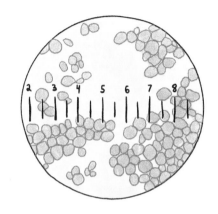

INTRODUCTION

There is a rush of excitement when checking in on a fresh batch of beer as it's fermenting—the anticipation of the unknown. The brew day went smoother than planned, and the yeast was pitched at the correct time and temperature. Even with all your careful measurements and diligence, you know it's the yeast itself that will determine whether this sweet, sticky liquid becomes a crisp, delicious brew to share with friends and family. Then, just like that, you hear it: *blip, blip, blip,* the welcome sound of vigorous fermentation.

There's a similar feeling when delving into bread making, between carefully weighing out ingredients, maybe even milling a locally grown flour, and kneading the dough ever so gently until it is nice and smooth—all with the hope of catching a glimpse of a bubble, oh wait there are two, emerging from the fermenting dough. These are the satisfying signs that yeast is doing what it's meant to do and that fresh hot bread is in your future.

It's said that brewers and bakers make wort and dough, but yeast is what actually makes beer and bread. Yeast is a single-cell organism, born out of a primordial soup. This tenacious microbe has arguably done more to elevate our cuisine by allowing humans to flourish from its fermentation by-products. It's produced and protected our food sources, even lending essential nutrients, such as B vitamins, to the diet of our ancestral Homo sapiens.

As humans evolved, so did yeast. There are hundreds of species and substrains. Even within the most common *Saccharomyces cerevisiae* species, there are variations, each as unique as a fingerprint, lending an array of delicious aromas and flavors. Humans have gone on to domesticate *Saccharomyces* subcolonies to harness those flavors, from the bubblegum- and clove-like Belgian to the clean biscuit characteristics of German lager yeast. English ales lend sweet esters such as pear and stone fruit, while Norwegian yeast impart soft rumlike citrus and sugarcane. Even American ales and lagers have come about through generations of ferments with their own complex tendencies. All that variety means the same recipe for bread or beer can yield vastly different characteristics simply by changing up the yeast. It's why for brewers and bakers, the world of yeast is full of possibilities.

This book looks under the microscope at the inner workings of this most fascinating and appetizing microorganism. Whether you've brewed a couple of times with a group of friends or have baked a few loaves of sourdough as a weekend activity, this book aims to help you better understand the ins and outs of yeast fermentation—and learn how to harness its powers in your crafting of breads and beers. Curious about the art of starters? Or maybe you want to see what happens to a beer when you switch up the carboy temperature. We've got easy-to-follow recipes and thought-provoking projects for them all. You'll also learn about the long history of yeast fermentation, from accidental discovery to purposeful experimentation.

Think of this book as your practical, in-depth guide to demystifying the secret life of yeast and putting deep fermentation know-how into practice in the kitchen and home brewery. Are you ready? The anticipation of bubbles and blips awaits.

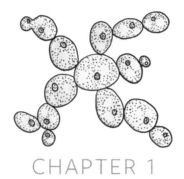

CHAPTER 1

WHAT IS YEAST?

Humans have been harnessing the power of yeast—for making beer and wine, baking bread, and fermenting foods—since the dawn of civilization. In fact, hieroglyphics show that the ancient Egyptians were using yeast as far back as 4000 BCE. It's not a stretch to say that yeast have helped humankind thrive through the ages. But what is yeast, and what exactly does it do?

THE FUNGUS AMONG US

Yeast are single-celled microorganisms that can be found everywhere on Earth: on animals and insects, on most vegetation (for example, the powdery-white surfaces of fruit such as grapes and dark stone fruits such as plums and sweet dates), in the air and water, and even on your skin. They also inhabit soil, can be found on most vegetation, and are prevalent in aquatic areas, such as oceans or lakes, with a burgeoning affinity for water.

There are more than 500 species of yeast that humans can cultivate. *Saccharomyces cerevisiae* (also known as baker's or brewer's yeast) is the most common. The Greek root *saccharo* means "sugar" (yeast feed on sugar) and *myces* means "fungus" (yeast are classified as members of the fungus kingdom). Yeast are, in fact, closely related to the mushrooms we use in day-to-day cooking and are the same fungi or molds used to ripen cheeses, pickle vegetables, ferment wine, and even produce antibiotics. On the funky end of the spectrum, *Brettanomyces*, a wild yeast discovered in Britain (hence the name) produces some of the more unique fermentation flavors. *Brett,* as it is affectionately named, has a voracious appetite and will eat basically everything. A beer fermented with *brett* will finish dry as all the residual sugar is gobbled up. It does best when competing with other strains and will clean up any unwanted by-products that may be left behind, such as the ropiness of *pediococcus*. In bread, *brett* will power through dormancy and ferment dough at low temperatures, enabling deep flavors to develop slowly.

Whatever the strain or variety—cultivated or wild—yeast all share the same complex internal cell structure as those found in plants and animals. They're round and spherical to ovular and ellipsoidal in shape. They can hang out by themselves or cluster together like grapes, even forming a small pyramid when they flocculate at the bottom of a carboy or when they go into hibernation. Sometimes they mate to make daughter cells; other times they make copies of themselves, giving yeast its characteristic peanut shape and leaving behind a small scar where the bud formed.

Believe it or not, there's a link between the reproductive proteins found in human cells and the reproductive proteins found in mating yeast cells. So much so that they have no problem being modified with human genes. It's even been theorized that some of the components found in human cells stem from a fusion of yeast cells, among others. With all these associations, it's no wonder that yeast is man's most endearing microbe. They've lived side by side with people for all of human history, gifting their food essential vitamins and preservative properties. In the early times of man, yeast protected water sources from harmful bacteria through its ability to grow fast and decrease the pH of water (dangerous alkaline-loving bacteria can't flourish in yeast-acidified waters).

In all, you could say that yeast have allowed humans not only to be sustained but thrive in a wild world: by helping to preserve food while enriching it with nutrients and flavors, protecting it from spoilage and harmful bacteria. Yeast have also undoubtedly given humans some of their simple enjoyments and pleasures—from gathering around the table with breads and pastries to sharing a pint that nourishes the community in more ways than one.

YEAST VS. BACTERIA

Those brand-new to fermentation projects sometimes confuse yeast with bacteria. Yeast are more closely related to humans than they are to bacteria, which are single cells with a stand-alone chromosome (as compared to yeast's 16 chromosomes).

Bacteria are almost always much smaller than yeast, and when they find their way into beer fermentation, they're most often considered an infection. Yet in sourdoughs, they're often thought of as delightfully acidic additions. Most commonly, *Lactobacilli* bacteria fermentation produces lactic acid instead of alcohol. Other bacterial fermentations can produce acetic acid, butyric acid, or even caprylic acid. In moderation, lactic acid, which is usually produced by bacteria, can add a nice acidity to sourdough bread. There are some bacteria that are harmful to bread, but since bread is baked, high oven temperatures will most likely kill them off.

In beer, bacteria such as *Pediococcus* is used in wild and sour fermentation, such as lambic. *Pediococcus* can also ruin beer styles like lagers, stouts, and IPAs. In this case, it's important for the brewer and baker to know how to protect against such bacteria. Although bacteria are not the focus of this book, it is smart to classify it so we can understand the differences between bacteria and yeast.

ANATOMY

To understand how yeast make fermentation happen in bread and beer, it's helpful to start with the nitty-gritty: the biology. After all, fermentation is an art and a science. Interestingly, yeast are composed of eight membrane-bound organelles suspended in cytoplasm that all contribute to the general health and stability of the cell. On a very basic level, picture a yeast cell as a full water balloon. The latex rubber of the balloon is much like a cell wall and the water like the cytoplasm, holding in suspension all the organelles so they can perform their functions. As fermenters, the baker or brewer's job is to grasp how a yeast cell's components work together to produce the by-products we seek in our beer and bread.

Nucleus

The nucleus is the brain of the cell, responsible for controlling its functions. Yeast contain 16 chromosomes in their nuclei (compared to 23 in humans) and can exist in a state where there is either one copy of the chromosomes (known as "haploid") or two copies of the chromosomes ("diploid"). You might remember from high school biology classes that the nucleus's main function is to house DNA, control gene expression, and replicate DNA during the cell cycle. When a yeast needs to produce a certain protein or enzyme that will be used for fermentation, the beginning of the production chain starts in the nucleus. It is not bound by a membrane, so it is not considered an organelle.

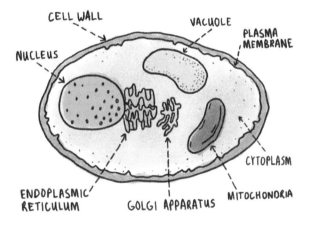

Endoplasmic Reticulum

Think of the endoplasmic reticulum as a yeast cell's spinal cord, the main channel through which messages are sent. Its primary function is to balance pH and store ions. There are two types of endoplasmic reticulum: one that's rough where protein is produced and one that's smooth where lipids or fats are produced. It may also house enzymes used to break down proteins for nutrition.

Golgi Apparatus

The Golgi apparatus is analogous to the nervous system in the human body. It is the dispatch station for proteins traveling from the endoplasmic reticulum to the cell surface.

Mitochondria

The mitochondria are like the energy factory or the power plant of the cell, serving the same function as our muscles. This is where glycolysis (the first step in the breakdown of glucose) and fermentation take effect. Some of the enzymes, such as alcohol dehydrogenase, leave the Golgi apparatus and make their way into the mitochondria to work on fermentation activities. Here at the mitochondria membrane, glycolysis primarily takes place (cellular respiration occurs inside the mitochondrial organelle). As glucose ferments, adenosine triphosphate is produced, giving the cell energy to perform its other functions, such as reproduction.

Vacuole

The vacuole functions much like a person's large intestine, breaking down proteins and ridding the yeast cell of waste. As the largest organelle in the cell, the vacuole's primary functions are pH and ion balance. It may house enzymes used to break down proteins for nutrition. Some of the enzymes, including those of the mitochondria, are sent to the vacuole when their functions are no longer acceptable. In the vacuole, the proteins or enzymes are broken down into their basic amino acid parts. Additionally, the vacuole can be used to hold venomous or undesirable cellular components in the yeast cell to protect the rest of the cell.

Cell Wall

The cell wall—the structural layer or skin of the yeast cell—functions a lot like the skin on the human body, protecting its contents from outside contaminants. Most of the cell wall consists of beta polysaccharide chains, fibrous β-1,6 glucan, and mannoproteins. Chitin is also considered a minor structural component in the cell wall, providing strength and support. These different components on the exterior surface are what make it quite impenetrable.

Plasma Membrane

Like your mouth and digestive track, allowing food in and out, the plasma membrane is the gateway between the cytoplasm and the cell wall. It performs a variety of functions, such as the free diffusion of solutes, selective uptake of substances, signal transduction, catalysis of reactions, energy storage, energy dissipation, binding sites for signaling pathways, and modulation of cell shape and polarity. The plasma membrane is made up of different lipids and protein species. The lipid components are broken down into phospholipids, glycophospholipids, and ergosterol. There are more than 2,000 membrane-bound proteins discovered, all peppered throughout the membrane to allow for efficient regulation in space and time.

Cytoplasm

The cytoplasm is a gel-like substance that consists of 80 to 85% water. The remaining 10 to 15% is proteins, 2 to 4% is lipids or fats, 1% is polysaccharides, and 1% are nucleic. The internal structure of a yeast cell, comprising the organelles, is much like a human cell. When the yeast are deprived of sugars, the cell's cytoplasm becomes acidic, which coagulates soluble proteins to make the cell less fluid. Acidic cytoplasm causes cellular activity to decrease for the cell to save its energy.

LIFE CYCLE

A yeast cell's life cycle spans from dormancy, activation, metabolism, reproduction, and growth, then back to dormancy or death, not unlike a perennial plant that returns every spring. The cell will grow, divide, and ultimately die or lie latent. Like a rose bush, it develops by receiving vital nutrients and energy, growing and thriving through a process known as budding. Where a rose bush will then flower and pollinate before dying back to the soil during dormancy, so, too, will yeast obtained in a dormant state. The yeast cell will move from activation to growth phase, using vital nutrients and sugar sources to go through fermentation and reproduction, then back to dormancy, awaiting its next cycle.

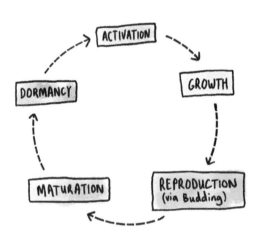

Dormancy

Lying asleep or as if asleep, the yeast cell patiently waits for the next part of its life cycle. Dormancy is a state of rest or inactivity. It is a minimal phase where metabolic activity will slow down or cease. This can be a reaction to adverse conditions or as a part of the organism's normal rhythm. Yeast cell dormancy is part of its natural life cycle and is usually temporary. For *Saccharomyces cerevisiae*, when food supplies are running short, yeast will stop dividing and toughen up their cell wall. The yeast will acidify their cytoplasm by releasing pH, decreasing molecules from their vacuole. The acidification of the cytoplasm will coagulate structural proteins in the yeast in order to make the cell more rigid and strengthen its cell wall. This is when the yeast cell enters hibernation. This will allow them to survive off whatever nutrients they have on reserve, even in the harshest of conditions, similar to the rose bush, which in the fall and winter months will lie dormant, withstanding the harsh winds and cold. With proper water and nutrients, it will survive this only to bloom again.

Activation and Inoculation

Microorganisms are introduced into an environment suited to their growth. When yeast is thrust out of dormancy into a new environment of freshly brewed wort or a mix of flour and water, they adjust to the surrounding temperature, sugar concentration, pH, environment composition, and level of dissolved oxygen.

Also known as the lag phase, at this time the yeast will begin to use their glycogen reserves, the way humans use their fat cells, in order to provide energy and create enzymes and sterols for the cell membrane. As mentioned before, oxygen is a necessary component in the construction of the cell wall and similar processes. This allows the membrane to control the passage of nutrients from bread or beer into the cell. During this time, the development of sterols in the cell membrane will allow the yeast stability to metabolize wort or grain sugars into alcohol and carbon dioxide without contributing off-flavors or off-odors.

To return to our analogy of a rose bush, this stage would be similar to germination, where the rose would start its early phases of growth. With the sun shining brighter and new vitamins and minerals being offered up, there might even be a couple of green sprouts on the bush.

Metabolism

At this stage, the cell's material substance is produced, maintained, and destroyed. This is where the energy that enables reproduction is made available. Once the yeast have equilibrated to their surrounding wort or starter, they can move on to a more expansive growth. The two basic steps to metabolism of simple sugars are glycolysis and the TCA cycle. Glycolysis, which is found right outside of the mitochondrial organelle, breaks down glucose into pyruvate. Then, if oxygen is present, the TCA cycle happens. This enables a bunch of energy-producing reactions and inhibits the production of alcohol. The TCA cycle produces carbon dioxide and energy, which is the ideal situation for bread making. If oxygen is not present, pyruvate moves into the alcohol fermentation process where it is converted into acetaldehyde and then to ethanol. Carbon dioxide is also produced but at a much lower level. Energy is obtained by glucose molecules in the wort or bread starter in order to make ATP in a process known as fermentation. During fermentation, sugar is converted into carbon dioxide and ethanol, or alcohol. Customarily, fermentation happens in the absence of oxygen. Accordingly, it is anaerobic by nature. Metabolism in yeast also refers to cell respiration in the absence of oxygen. Carbon dioxide is then released as a cell waste or by-product. Unlike actual waste, carbon dioxide and ethanol are actually very valuable. These two items are what make bread, beer, and all fermented products so special.

This process is parallel to the rose bush in its growth stage. The small sprouts will start building up energy and reserves to prepare for reproduction or budding.

Reproduction

As a member of the fungus family, yeast can reproduce both asexually and sexually. The former process is called "budding"—diploid cells "bud" off from each other to make daughter cells. The latter method is via "mating" (stimulated by a phero-mone)—two haploid cells fuse to form a diploid daughter cell. Cell division occurs about every 90 minutes, meaning that during a 100-hour typical fermentation, you can see up to 10,000 progeny per cell. The mother is left with a bud scar, a chitinous craterlike ring. Unlike a human daughter, who has half of her mom's DNA, yeast cell reproduction is more akin to plant bud-ding, containing a twin copy of its mother's DNA. The rose bush at this point will bud and be pol-linated. This creates the prize of its life cycle: a beautiful rose.

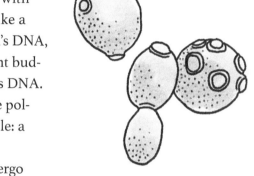

Haploid yeast cells may first need to undergo mating to form a diploid daughter cell before the budding process takes place. This occurs more commonly under high-stress conditions where sporulation must occur. Mating is stimulated by a pheromone and is thought to be the primary selective force in maintaining an enhanced recombinational repair of DNA damage during meiosis among extremely similar yeast progeny. The recur-ring diploid daughter now has the chance to align the chromosomes and see which are matches and which are erroneous and fix them. In this way, the yeast can correct mutations within itself.

Dormancy or Death

Once yeast use up all nutritional molecules, the cell will revert back to dormancy: It stores energy in its glycogen, the cell walls harden, and the cell becomes latent once again. Death can occur through autolysis or self-digestion (the destruction of the cell by its own enzymes), by exposure to extreme heat or cold, or in environments that are too wet or too dry. Yeast can also be harmed by invading bacteria (see page 48), which can leave them "sick." However, it is very difficult to kill yeast. While it may seem like yeast are dead or not viable, with proper care, they can usually be coaxed out of dormancy. Like a rose bush, dormancy would be its state during the winter months in which the plant is still alive but not producing any flowers. Death would be when the rose bush dies or is self-digested and will not produce flowers the coming spring.

WHAT YEAST NEEDS

During dormancy, a yeast cell needs very little nutrition to maintain stasis. During active states (metabolism, growth, reproduction, or fermentation), however, yeast need a variety of sugars, amino acids, nitrogen compounds, and cofactors to fuel their development.

One of the critical factors to cell development is a hospitable environment: Yeast function best in warm, moist surroundings. They need moisture to begin metabolizing the nutrients that are essential for them to thrive. A comfortable temperature encourages yeast to grow and multiply. In the proper conditions, with the correct amounts of sugars, minerals, vitamins, yeast should grow rapidly and easily. The following nutrients are also needed:

Vitamins: Biotin (B7), folic acid (B9), inositol, niacin (B3), pantothenate (B5), pyridoxine (B6), riboflavin (B2), and thiamin (B1) are essential for yeast activity.

Fatty acids: Fatty acids make up the components of the cell membrane. They are responsible for the cell's structure, leading to its capacity to consume sugar.

Nitrogen: Nitrogen compounds are the second most important nutrient for yeast besides sugar (see description for sugars), directly impacting its ability to grow and multiply.

Minerals: Yeast require minerals such as zinc and potassium for basic cellular function and growth.

Sugars: Yeast need a supply of energy to grow and thrive. Through a process called "glycolysis," they generate energy from sugars (glucose, maltose, galactose, and fructose). The by-products of this process are ethanol (alcohol) and carbon dioxide, which are imperative for brewing and baking.

CHAPTER 2

THE ULTIMATE KITCHEN HELPERS

Yeast has long been a part of humanity's culinary traditions, going back thousands of years. In this chapter, we look at the fascinating ways humans have used yeast throughout history—and how modern brewers and bakers use yeast today.

A NARRATIVE HISTORY

It starts at dusk in the ancient city of Thinis. An Egyptian woman sits on the ground, preparing to grind dried wheat to make bread for her family's dinner. She places the wheat in a large clay bowl, then, using a heavy stone, starts grinding it in strong, swift yet graceful motions. It is backbreaking work. Once the grain is finely ground into flour, she sifts it carefully using a sieve to rid it of debris. She then lights a fire in her clay oven (similar to what is now known as a tandoor) and proceeds to make her dough. Adding water to the freshly ground flour, she mixes the dough and then kneads it into smooth, flat rounds. She places them on the outside layer of the hot oven to cook. The bread she is making will be dense and flat, much like modern-day pita.

While the bread is baking, she starts making beer. She takes some of the partially baked bread from the oven and crumbles it into a jar of water. She adds raw date honey, which is naturally yeast-laden, and mixes the concoction. She then leaves it to sit and transform into a light bubbly liquid.

Egyptian beer was not unlike the traditional modern-day Lithuanian beer known as *keptinis,* in which the mash is first baked in the oven until it forms a thick crust. It is then cooled and crushed or crumbled to a coarse meal. This meal is mashed again before strained into a large fermentation vessel. The vessel is then covered, and the mixture is left alone to ferment. Opinions differ on whether yeast was added or if the fruits or sweeteners had yeast on them naturally.

The Egyptian woman making the beer and bread, of course, didn't fully understand that all this was happening because of yeast and fermentation. (Hieroglyphics more than 5,000 years old depict bread and alcoholic beverages as magical, mysterious gifts from the gods.) In truth, yeast was all around the Egyptian woman—on the wheat grains themselves in the form of *Lactobacillus* and on raw date honey or the skins of fruit in the form of *Saccharomyces* or *Brettanomyces*.

The Hymn of Ninkasi

About 1,000 years later, in 1800 BCE, the lyrical poem "Hymn of Ninkasi" celebrates Sumerian brewing and is often thought to be one of the earliest records of fermented beverages, this time in what is present-day Iraq. Ninkasi was the Sumerian goddess of beer, guardian of brewers, and protector of the recipe. She would ensure the best quality of beer. Folklore proclaims that she was born out of sparkling water and tasked with satisfying all desires and satiating the heart of man.

The hymn of Ninkasi was sung by Sumerian brewers and bakers, who chanted the hymn or recipe over and over until it was forged in memory. The women would make a barley bread called *bappir*, a twice-baked concoction hard enough to be stored for long periods. It was also used to make a kind of beer that looked more like a sweet porridge elixir. It was poured into a bowl and enjoyed with a wide-mouthed straw. The women would save a small portion and use it in a batch of bread and beer—like today's sourdough or beer starters. After many uses, these starter cultures helped to select favorable yeast used to inoculate the next batch of bread and beer. Indeed, this early process of yeast selection helped shape the modern way people nourish yeast for their consumption.

Under the Microscope

Fast-forward to the 1700s, to the city of Delft in the Netherlands. In a dimly lit room, a pale gaunt man with a long curly wig and a lengthy coat is hunched over a microscope. Antonie van Leeuwenhoek was a successful Dutch textile merchant, scientist, and lens maker who built his own microscopes. Examining everything he could get his hands on—soil, leaves, water, his own blood—he was the first to observe and record single-cell organisms that he named "animalcules" (what we now call "microorganisms").

Van Leeuwenhoek came from a long line of *drapers,* or textile merchants and brewers. It may have been the call of his beer-making ancestors rooted inside him that led him to observe the world around him on a microscopic level. At the time, brewers still did not understand exactly how the combination of malted barley, hops, and water transformed into beer. They did recognize, however, that the cloudy substance that formed in beer after fermenting was responsible for producing their desired outcome, and so they would save the sludge and add it to the next batch.

When van Leeuwenhoek examined beer at different stages, what he observed was so unlike the diminutive rod-shaped cells (bacteria) he was used to seeing under his microscope. Small globular mounds would stick together and aggregate into larger groups. Although van Leeuwenhoek didn't recognize them for their worth, he was the first person to examine yeast up close and personal. Van Leeuwenhoek was so obsessed with the beer cells that he would draw them in his journal and even mold their shape out of wax. Thanks to his work, van Leeuwenhoek is now known as the Father of Microbiology.

Even though van Leeuwenhoek was on the right track, he failed to recognize yeast as a living organism or see its contribution in the making of beer. It would be another 150 years until a French baron and scientist named Charles Canard-Latour described the air bubbles in beer as being carbon dioxide and recognized that the globular mounds were not simply aggregating together but growing.

Finally, in the late 1800s, Louis Pasteur discovered (along with the principles of vaccination and pasteurization) that yeast was a true living organism—one with a star role in beer and bread making. And it's all because the wine-making father of one of Pasteur's students asked the scientist why his beet wine would sour. When Pasteur put the wine under a microscope, he saw large budding yeast and tiny bacterial contaminants. In turn, he isolated the larger yeast cells from the smaller bacterial cells, fed the samples sugar, and found the large yeast cells had turned the sugar into alcohol and the small bacterial cells turned the sugar into lactic acid. In doing so, he demonstrated that yeast was the agent responsible for alcoholic fermentation and dough leavening. Pasteur clearly defined yeast's role for brewers and bakers everywhere.

MODERN POWER BALLS

Contemporary yeast fermentation projects are vast. Of course, there is beer and bread, the star subjects of this book, but there are many other uses for yeast ranging from the common to obscure. Fermentation can take many forms and include a multitude of fungi and bacteria. Many alcoholic beverages include yeast and fermentation to convert sugar into alcohol, such as wine, kvass, kombucha, whiskey, mead, vodka, gin, bourbon, and tequila, to name a few. Depending on the recipe, different techniques and cultures produce different flavors, textures, and aromas. The area where each technique originated, as well as the ingredients available in that region, has a lot to do with which yeast culture was used in fermentation.

Wine

In today's wine making, *Saccharomyces* is the species of choice—mostly because of its predictability and vigorous fermentation capabilities. However, classically, the yeast used was more likely *Brettanomyces,* which is found on the skins of grapes or even at the bottom of feet. After crushing the grapes, stems, and leaves, the wild yeast would work to break down carbohydrates in grapes, which are abundant in natural sugars. The slightly tart and funky taste that *Brettanomyces* imparts in naturally fermented wine may not be what modern palates are accustomed to, but it's a truly complex and interesting experience. Of course, today, with the help of clean practices and sterilization, *Saccharomyces* is used to make a more consistent and tame product.

In most modern wineries, if *Brettanomyces* is detected, the barrel is quickly disposed of and all equipment is promptly sterilized or replaced. *Brettanomyces* is said to give an off-flavor in wine that can taste like bandages. In high concentrations, it can indeed leave a red wine smelling like old gym socks. On the other hand, in small concentrations, *Brettanomyces* might add a wonderful complexity to naturally fermented or wild yeast wines. There are many vintners who are now experimenting with this yeast to make wild and naturally fermented wine that's more readily available for purchase. It's also a favorite home project to share with friends.

Distilled Liquor

Distiller's yeast is commonly used in extremely high-gravity beverages, with a 15 to 18% alcohol content. The mash is fermented until peak attenuation, usually 18% alcohol. The resulting liquor is called *wash*. Distillers then take the wash and distill it through columns; the resulting distilled liquor is called spirit. Liquor such as vodka is made this way and can be flavored to make gin or absinthe. Some of these spirits are aged in oak casks to add flavor and complexity—the result would be bourbon, whiskey, scotch, or rye. Distiller's yeast has a higher alcohol tolerance than standard beer yeast. It is a champagne varietal *Saccharomyces* with added nutrients, so it can withstand high temperatures and high alcohol. The nutrients added to distiller's yeast are DAP (diammonium phosphate), zinc, and free ammoniums. These help stimulate multiplication and metabolism and decrease sulfur conjugate off-flavors. They are directly associated with the qualitative health of the yeast and its ability to grow and withstand high-volatile alcohols.

Bread, Beer, and Beyond

Aspergillus oryzae, or *koji,* is classified as *fungi* and is commonly used for fermentation in Japan. The Japanese heritage of fermentation is a rich tradition that has been going on for more than 2,000 years. This unique and refined process concentrates mostly on soy and rice to make interesting delicacies such as *miso*, a salty paste used in soups to add a deep flavor, and *shoyu*, a similar product to soy sauce with a more full-bodied flavor and delicate sweetness. Just like sourdough, *miso* and *shoyu* will vary in flavor and aroma depending on the region's agriculture and climate, and even the hands that are nurturing them.

There is also *nato*, a fermented bean with a distinct stringy character almost like cheese. *Amazake* is a traditional low-alcohol drink made by adding *koji* to cooked and cooled whole-grain rice. This causes the enzymes to break down the carbohydrates into simple unrefined sugars. In this process, sweetness develops naturally, but often sugar is added to the taste of the maker. *Koji,* or *tsukemono,* are pickled vegetables with an extra umami tone and a hint of sweetness. Although still obscure in the West, these intriguing and complex flavors are becoming more popular. Technically a mold, koji has greatly influenced the cuisine of fermentation around the world, in which it is used to quicken dry-aging steak and other meat products. There are even experimental brewers and bakers at home and in professional settings who are using koji instead of *Saccharomyces* strains to make something truly new and wonderful.

There is an old adage that says, people don't make bread and beer; yeast does. Brewers make wort, a syrupy, viscous liquid full of nutrient-rich carbohydrates and sugars. This is the perfect home for yeast to thrive and turn wort into beer. Bakers mix dough and, through time and temperature, create the ideal environment for yeast to transform the glutinous concoction into bread.

Early on, yeast have conditioned (some may even say domesticated) humans to care for them, perhaps for their own replicative gains. In return, yeast give humans the gift of alcohol and the sustenance of bread. Clearly, humans have benefited greatly from this exchange. The human gut metabolizes yeast's volatile and short-chain fatty acids into B vitamins—B6 and B12 are crucial factors in blood-cell production and stability and stave off conditions such as megaloblastic anemia or pellagra—and vitamin K,

YEAST THROUGH THE AGES

When you think about it, it's amazing that humans used yeast for thousands of years without ever realizing its existence or function. And although it is unclear which came first—bread or beer—the two have been inextricably tied since ancient civilization.

80 million years ago yeast comes into existence.

4000 BCE Ancient Egyptians and Sumerians bake bread and brew beer.

150 BCE First bakers' guild is established in ancient Rome.

1676 Antonie van Leeuwenhoek peers into the microscope and sees yeast for the first time.

1762 Michael Combrune, a London brewer, realizes yeast is essential for brewing beer.

1818 Johann Christian Polycarp Erxleben, a German naturalist, describes yeast as vegetable matter responsible for fermentation.

1837 Theodor Schwann, a German biologist, describes yeast as fungus.

1838 Franz Julius Ferdinand Meyen, a Prussian physician and botanist, gives yeast the name *Saccharomyces*.

1859 Louis Pasteur discovers how yeast work.

1880 Emil Christian Hansen, director of the Carlsberg brewing laboratory in Denmark, isolates single yeast cells for pure culture pitches—aka single-strain yeast volumes.

1903 Niels Hjelte Claussen classifies *Brettanomyces* at Carlsberg brewing laboratories.

1908 Emil Christian Hansen isolates the lager strain, which at the time was considered the best yeast for brewing beer.

1942 Fleischmann laboratories in New York develop active dry yeast.

1973 Lesaffre in France develops instant dry yeast. This marked a major advance, eliminating the constraints associated with rehydrating active dry yeast.

1984 Fleischmann laboratories develops rapid rise yeast, which causes dough to rise 50% faster than active dry yeast.

1996 Yeast genome is sequenced by the National Institute of Health.

2019 Researchers at the University of California genetically modify yeast to produce the cannabinoids THC and CBD.

which promotes healthy blood clotting. Vitamin K has also been described as supporting bone structure formation and overall brain function, preventing heart attack, stroke, and clotting diseases.

Perhaps those benefits are the hidden gems of the love and consumption of yeast. Bread and beer are basically the same, with almost identical ingredients and flavor profiles. Beer is often referred to as liquid bread and bread as baked beer. In fact, biochemically, the processes in beer and bread are very similar. Through the use of grain-based starch or dextrinous mediums to extract sugars, either via bacterial efforts or heat, those sugars are then fermented in a specific way to capture either alcohol in beer or carbon dioxide in bread.

For fermentation fans, the crafting of beer and bread is the perfect marriage of art and science. Yeast can be engineered to produce beer and bread via specific mechanisms and well-described processes, but this will not guarantee a tasty loaf or brew on its own. When it comes to the delicate essence and exotic ingredients used in these recipes—not to mention the microflora and -fauna of distinct regions and the multiple combinations thereof—what we have is very much an art-driven practice. And the artist, naturally, is the baker and brewer, each with their own technique, imagination, experience, and palate to blend ingredients together to make one-of-a-kind creations.

WHAT YEAST DOES FOR BREAD + BEER

Make no mistake: Fermentation is a well-described and well-documented science. In short, yeast metabolize a simple sugar source into alcohol and carbon dioxide. You might have already guessed, though, that the finer mechanisms are far more complex and vast, but in this section we'll break it all down into a simple thread of ideas.

First, the human factor: Whether you're baking or brewing, your role is to break down starches and proteins into usable sugars and amino acids for yeast to metabolize. You've just ground your malt bill and poured it into a large pot or a *mash tun*. It's

20TH-CENTURY DISCOVERIES

Yeast have been used as vehicles for medicinal production since the beginning of the industry, taking the place of mammalian cell lines in producing key proteins essential in biological functions. In more recent years, these cultures have helped produce many medicines, including vaccines, insulin, and plasminogen activators. In fact, insulin production in yeast is hailed as one of the most important findings of the 20th century, allowing more than a million diabetics affordable and efficient therapy.

A recent study also found that genetically modified yeast can produce the biomedical active compounds found in cannabis, THC and CBD. These compounds show a variety of therapeutic uses, including anti-anxiolytic properties, anti-inflammatory results, and even implications in severe chronic conditions, such as cancer and heart disease.

Another industry that's made the most of this amazing organism is biofuel. Genetically modified yeast can resist alcohol concentration and immense heat in order to produce fuel that cars and power plants run on. In theory, the use of these new biofuels will allow the world to cut down on coal usage as well as oil and gas consumption. Indeed, this very green organism has proven its versatility and usefulness in our modern world.

time to mash in, a process that turns the malted barley into a sugary wort that activates enzymes through heat. This sticky liquid will later be the food the yeast will transform into what everyone knows and loves: beer. This is akin to a baker's process during the fermentation and proofing of their dough—either by using a high-gluten flour with enough proteins for the yeast to metabolize or by adding a diastatic malt to give that extra sugar content. Through proper time and temperature, yeast will metabolize these sugars and create carbon dioxide. Carbon dioxide production will ultimately be the deciding factor on the final rise and flavor of the bread.

AMYLOPECTIN → AMYLOSE

Starches to Simple Sugar

To begin—what is a starch and what is a simple sugar? Starch is a long chain hydrocarbon, a chain of carbon atoms bonded to hydrogen atoms. Starches have many hydrocarbon chains and rings linked to its main backbone. Glucose, or simple sugar, is the most important source of energy in all organisms. When a baker or brewer buys a whole grain, whether it is barley or wheat, the carbohydrate energy source is in the form of a long chain hydrocarbon, as shown in the picture below. Each ring is highly dense and unexposed for the yeast to do its bidding.

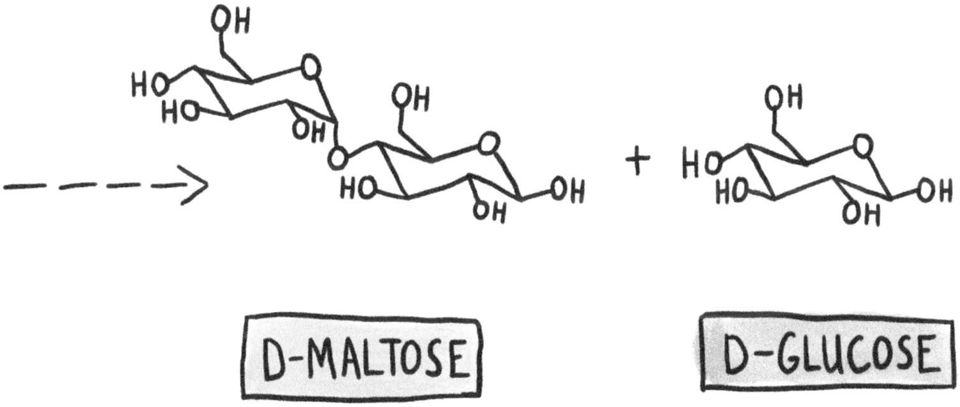

D-MALTOSE

D-GLUCOSE

Imagine trimming a tree from very complex branches down to minimal sticks for easy cleanup. That's exactly what the baker and brewer need to do: knead or mash the grains in order to break the chains into simpler and simpler molecules until a simple sugar ring is all that remains. The enzymes brewers use in the mashing process are developed in the grain kernel during the germination stage; enzymes are then crystallized during the malting process. Once a brewer mills the malt, they mash in with hot water, and the heat activates the enzymes (such as amylase, cellulase, protease, and glucanase) to break down starches and long chain sugars into simple monosaccharides. In the case of the baker, the grain is milled and mixed with room-temperature water, kneaded, and proofed to activate the enzymes and break down the starches.

This is done through hydrolysis of hydrocarbon chains by the use of heat and enzymes trapped in the grain kernels. For the brewer, a mash is heated to 154°F (67°C), whereas a baker achieves this by proper kneading or by placing the dough in a warm room or proofer. Yeast love simple sugars, such as glucose, fructose, sucrose, maltose, and maltotriose.

Simple Sugar to Alcohol + Carbon Dioxide

Once you have provided your microbial helper with a suitable food source, yeast in turn ferments these simple sugar rings into alcohol and carbon dioxide for you. The conversion of glucose sugars into alcohol and carbon dioxide follows a process known as glycolysis and respiration. Yeast use these mechanisms with the help of enzymatic phosphatases and dehydrogenases to produce energy in the form of ATP for itself—and in the process, alcohol and carbon dioxide for the brewer or baker.

There are many simple sugars yeast will happily fill up on—glucose being the most common. It's found in the mash of malted barley and/or the pre-ferment of wheat used in bread making and brewing. Maltose and maltotriose, which yeast also love, are a result of the same processes. Other sources of glucose include maple syrup and honey.

Sucrose and fructose found in fruit, such as grapes and apples, are readily available to be consumed by yeast on a whim. Sucrose is a major chemical component of simple table sugar that can be added to bread as well as the more complex Belgian candy sugars, most commonly used in the Belgian brewing tradition.

When glucose reaches the yeast cellular membrane, glucose-specific transmembrane transport proteins usher in glucose molecules into the cytosol of the cell. Once inside, the glucose molecule will make its way to the mitochondria for glycolysis and respiration to occur. Glycolysis of glucose to pyruvate, via phosphorylation, happens at the perimeter of the mitochondrial membrane. Pyruvate then travels into the mitochondria where it is converted to acetaldehyde and then further into ethanol by alcohol dehydrogenases. Ethanol and carbon dioxide (relatively small molecules) then seep through the plasma membrane and out of the cells, giving the medium its bubbly character.

Structure + Texture

Bread

Bread's structure and texture is the result of the building of gluten. There are a few ways to form gluten in bread. Starting out with a high-gluten bread flour will help in this process, as will kneading dough. By kneading the dough repeatedly, gliadin and glutenin proteins in the flour expand and create stretchy gluten strands, which give bread its risen structure and chewy texture. The dough is warmed by the kneading process, transforming the slack original mixture into a springy, elastic concoction with pockets of carbon dioxide gas, created by the yeast and trapped in the glutinous matrix.

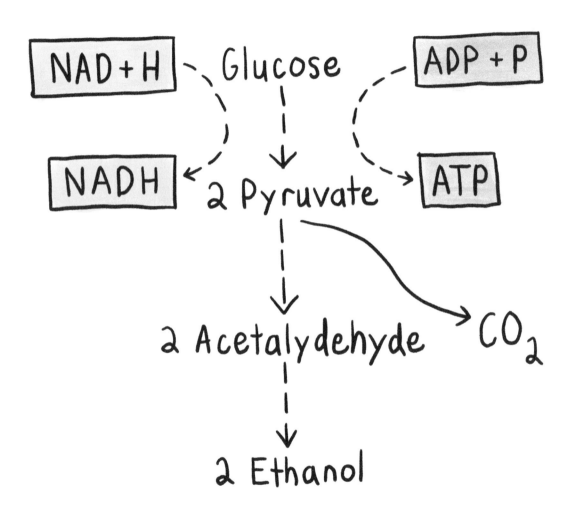

If kneading goes well, it will result in a light, fluffy bread with beautiful oven spring. A dough that is heavily kneaded will have a multitude of tiny air bubbles densely packed together and be soft to the touch. It will spring back when pressed and have a substantial mouthfeel. A dough that does not have sufficient gluten built up will be flat and gummy.

Folding is another method to build gluten in bread. This process is much gentler and is usually used in naturally fermented and high-hydration doughs with long fermentation periods. Folding is done by taking one side of the dough and stretching it to the other end—then doing it again until all four sides are folded on top of each other like an envelope. There are many different folding techniques, each rendering its desired outcome for variously hydrated doughs. Folding is usually repeated every half hour, hour, or two hours for a total of four to six hours. By folding the dough, layers will be created to trap carbon dioxide and disperse the yeast. The end result will be a bread with uniform large to medium air pockets throughout the crumb. The crust will be thick and crunchy, while the center will be soft and chewy.

Beer

Beer has little structure except for mouthfeel and carbonation, which will give a perceived structure and texture. Mouthfeel is dictated by residual dextrins left over from the mash, and glycerin, a by-product of yeast reproduction. The mouthfeel will determine the body of a beer, impacting a beer's drinkability. The use of oats and unmodified wheat varieties will create a more dextrinous beer with a silky, creamy, or thick mouthfeel (think wheat beer or oatmeal stout).

A lager with a high glycerin production, even with crisp carbonation, can have a substantial, chewy mouthfeel. Beer fermented with baker's varieties of yeast retains very little glycerin and therefore leads to a thin or cidery mouthfeel. In fermented beverages, where the sugar sources are high and the amino acid sources are low, cellular reproduction will be sluggish and there will be minimal glycerin production, hence the term cidery to describe a watery, insubstantial beer with a thin mouthfeel.

Carbonation is determined by the level of carbon dioxide dissolved and trapped in a liquid. Carbonation levels will dictate the effervescence and the reaction of flavor compounds on the tongue with every sip. That bubbly, tingling feeling in your mouth as you let the liquid linger will have a lot to do with your overall impression of the beer. Lower carbonation will bring out more malty or caramel-like flavors. A low-carbonated beverage will appear fuller and slicker. Stout, a beer style that is famous for its medium- to full-bodied mouthfeel, is less carbonated and served at a warmer temperature. This is an example of a beer that is still desirable and delicious when the carbonation levels are low. It can be velvety with an almost oily slickness. A high-carbonation beer will bring out more floral and fruity flavors, along with acids—it will feel lighter and sparkling. Berliner Weisse, for example, has a light body and very high carbonation levels. This effervescent beverage is crisp and juicy with light acidity.

Malted Barley ------> MASHING Wort (Glucose, Maltose Dextrose, and Maltotriose) -----> GLYCOLYSIS IN YEAST Pyruvate ---> Pyruvic Flavor Compounds (Caramel, Rum, Floral)

CO_2

Acetaldehyde ---> Acetyl Flavor Compounds (Green Apple, Vinegar, Butter Popcorn)

FERMENTATION

ATP

Alcohol

Alcohol Spikes

Let's be honest: Beer would not be as popular as it is without the alcohol. It adds to mouthfeel, body, flavor, and aroma, and is the reason why beer is so much fun to drink. For the brewer, alcohol production is the driving focus of the work. In order to produce the best wort for yeast fermentation, the brewer has to keep in mind quite a few things. For example, sugar extraction and conversion dictate fermentability of wort. Mashing in at too-high or too-low temperatures or caramelizing sugar in the boil kettle can lead to inaccessible sugars and an overtly sweet or thin beer. This is why it's so important to hit your numbers for your sugar concentration and temperatures. Whether it be for a low-alcohol or high-alcohol content, being exact in this process is critical. Alcohol resistance and attenuative properties of a yeast culture are among some of the factors that lead to the concentration of alcohol in beer. Of course, the amount of sugar added plays a huge role in yeast ability to produce more alcohol; fermentation time doesn't necessarily predict the alcohol content in a beer.

High-alcohol content in a beer can be used to thin out the body and give it a lighter mouthfeel. In a high-gravity imperial stout, the amount of alcohol is in place to thin out the viscosity. Alcohol can also impart a fruit-forward flavor and aroma. In a Belgian golden strong ale, high-alcohol fruitiness complements the Belgian bubble-gum and banana profile produced by the yeast.

Interestingly, the average beer has 5.5% alcohol, which gives a medium to low body and mouthfeel, characteristically balanced flavor, and lightly fruited aroma. Beers with too little alcohol or nonalcoholic beers can be very watery and thin bodied—they taste flat and, well, unexciting.

Meanwhile, the baker looks for *just* the right amount of alcohol when it comes to fermentation. Too much alcohol in bread baking or in the proofing cycle can inhibit yeast and bacteria from doing their job. The more sugar and more proofing time leads to an enhanced fermentation that will produce more carbon dioxide. The problem is if there is too much sugar or time, the carbon dioxide will escape and seep out of the dough leaving it flat and lifeless. This could also lead to unwanted tearing in the final dough, which can be seen after the final shape or in the bake. If there is too little time and sugar, the yeast will produce a minimal amount of carbon dioxide, fermentation will be stalled, and the dough will not be able to rise properly.

However, the alcohol yeast produce at the same time as carbon dioxide does lend to the flavor of dough. Most describe the taste as a fruit-forward complexity or having a fermentation quality. When too much alcohol is produced, it can have a vinous characteristic and leave the bread tasting like spirits or even vinegar. When there is too little alcohol produced, the dough will have the flavor of Play-Doh or glue.

Flavor Bombs

Big molecules in proteins, fatty acids, or starches taste muddy and gummy. Broken down, their building blocks (such as amino acids, esters, fusel alcohols, and sulfur-containing compounds) will have an impact on flavor, which you can control through technique and recipes.

Fermentation brings out all these permutations in bread and beer. Along with the conversion of sugar to alcohol, there are a myriad of flavor compounds released by yeast into the medium. When yeast are breaking down grains and sugars to make beer, you get phenols and esters. Phenols are generally a by-product of fermentation found predominantly in Belgian styles of beer. They lend a flavor and aroma of pepper, banana, and clove. Esters are flavor molecules commonly found in English ales, with notes of pear, apple, and stone fruits. In lambics and sour ales, there are many various acidic conjugates, such as acidic acid, which lends a malt vinegar–like flavor, and lactic acid, similar to a slightly tart kefir.

In bread, the large molecules in the flour are broken down into smaller flavorful ones. Enzymes encourage all kinds of reactions that break big chains of molecules into smaller ones: amylose and maltose into glucose, and proteins into amino acids. As fermentation proceeds, the dough tends to become more acidic, as in a sourdough. This is due in part by rising levels of carbon dioxide, but there are more flavorful organic compounds at play, such as lactic acid. Lactic acid has the familiar taste of plain yogurt and is a by-product of glucose metabolism. This acidity causes more molecules to break down and can leave the bread tasting overly sour and dense if taken too far.

THE SCIENCE OF TASTE

Taste buds located on the tongue are sensory epithelial cells. They are shaped like a feather or palm branch. When flavor molecules hit the palm branch–like structures in the mouth, a chemical reaction sparks. These sensory cells transmit a signal through the cranial nerves to the brain, and brain cells translate the sensation into taste. The varying shapes, locations, and strengths of receptance dictate the flavor intensity and nuances. There are also pressure receptors within the mouth that detect and influence mouthfeel, texture, and carbonation.

CHAPTER 3

PITCHING + HANDLING

Yeast can be capricious and mysterious, especially when you think about all the conditions it needs for fermentation. Like every species, it requires a delicate balance of time and space. For success, a baker or brewer must control the yeast's environment with great care, creating the right conditions around temperature, nutrients, oxygen, time, microbiomal co-cultures, and fermentation history.

HOSPITABLE HABITATS

Environment means almost everything to a yeast cell. Despite the fact that once activated, some type of fermentation is bound to happen, the success of your bake or brew depends on the happiness of this microorganism. The first step, as mentioned, is to bring it out of dormancy. A yeast cell in dormancy is alive but will not give you a desirable outcome. Hospitable habitats for baking and brewing are different (as are the likes and dislikes of *Saccharomyces* and *Brettanomyces*)—but are worth mastering. The variables and the ability to differentiate between them will be explained in this chapter.

Bread

Knowing exactly when yeast or a sourdough starter is viable to use in bread making can seem perplexing at times. It can be like searching for just-right conditions that seem wholly out of your control. Active dried yeast or instant rapid rise yeast are two of the most common yeast used by home bakers. It's also possible to buy bricks of fresh yeast in supermarkets—though it helps to call ahead of time to see if your store stocks it.

Active Dry Yeast

Most likely, the most common type of yeast you'll find at the market is active dry yeast. First, you dissolve the active dry yeast in water. To see if your yeast is alive, add a pinch of table sugar to the dissolved water and yeast mixture. In a couple minutes, the yeast will start to metabolize the sugar, and carbon dioxide will release. This will drive yeast out of latency and give it some initial momentum to kick-start fermentation. You'll see bubbles and a foamy layer form on top of the water. This means your yeast is viable and ready to start mixing into dough. If there is no change or activity seen, the yeast has died.

Instant Rapid Rise Yeast

Instant rapid rise yeast is often substituted for active dry yeast—teaspoon for teaspoon—and can be added straight to the measured-out flour. The only trouble is it's tougher to judge if the culture is still viable. If the yeast is indeed alive, there may be no signs of activity until the first bulk fermentation. However, if the yeast has been stored cold in the refrigerator or freezer, chances of success are greater. On the other hand, if the yeast was stored at room temperature, it becomes imperative to do these tests. You can also check for bubbles in a yeast, water, and sugar solution with instant rapid rise yeast (as a swap for active dry yeast).

Fresh Yeast

It's a little harder to find in grocery stores, but fresh yeast is another option that works well with this test: Soft and malleable, it can be substituted for active dry yeast or instant rapid rise yeast by three times the amount in weight.

Sourdough Starter

Sourdough is a different animal. It plays by a different set of rules than commercial yeast. Sourdough starter is a wonderful way to leaven (or let rise) bread, but it can take many hours to see if the starter is active or not. Patience is key, but it's worth it when you consider how hard it is to kill a sourdough starter. Most of the time, death is assumed when the starter has actually just dropped into latency. It will merely take a couple of feedings to reignite a dormant starter. A ripe starter will be light and fluffy to the touch with visible air bubbles. A simple test to see if your sourdough starter is ready is to place it in room-temperature water and see if it floats (a healthy one will).

Beer

Likewise, in the brewing process, it's important to examine yeast every step of the way to see how to best take care of the starter or culture. Yeast can be fickle, and it's the brewer's challenge to adhere to all the protocols and best practices. Many brewers use dehydrated yeast cells dried into dormancy—they're often available in home-brew and online stores. Others will use liquid starter that has grown up in wort.

Dehydrated Yeast

For the brewer, it is much more difficult to tell if dehydrated cultures are ready to pitch because they won't start fermenting for 24 hours. The anticipation can be vexing. Once fermentation has started, though, you'll see movement in the blowoff tube or airlock. The blipping sound of a fermenting wort can also be heard—even from another room.

Liquid Yeast

A liquid yeast starter is much easier to gauge. Similar to a sourdough starter, you will need patience for this process. You can start with a dehydrated yeast culture or liquid yeast from any professional yeast laboratory and mix it with a liter of wort. Swirl it around and let it sit for 48 hours. After, you'll start to see *krausen,* which is a foamy head that develops on top of fermenting beer. This culture is now ready to pitch into a beer!

There are many stages of fermentation in which proper yeast management is key to a productive outcome. Everything that touches the yeast culture to the fermenting wort must be sanitized or sterilized in every stage of the brewing process. This means equipment and vessels as well as your hands. Temperature is a tremendous factor too. Keeping the proper temperature—according to your recipe—for your culture's environment can mean the difference between success and failure.

KEY FERMENTATION FACTORS
FOR BEER AND BREAD

Factor	Too Low	Too High
Temperature	Yeast will go into dormancy and not kick into active fermentation.	Yeast will be active but produce off-flavors, mostly fusel alcohols, phenols, and esters. In dough, yeast will be overactive and CO_2 will escape, causing the dough to be flat.
Time	Fermentation will not be complete, and by-product flavor compounds, such as diacetyl, will stick around. Dough will not rise, and beer will not finish.	Yeast will undergo autolysis and give off soapy flavors in beer. Dough will go flat and stale.
Nutrients	Fermentation will be sluggish or develop off-flavors, such as diacetyl, ethyl acetate, or isoamyl acetate.	Although yeast love an abundance of nutrients, your beer or bread will not. Flavors of those nutrients will seep into the flavor of the bread or beer.
Oxygen	Yeast will not have the ability to form sterol components for their cell walls. Reproduction will not occur, and fermentation will be sluggish and stressed.	Yeast will produce more oxidative fermentation compounds, and flavors will be acetate- (acetone) forward.

WHY ISN'T THIS WORKING?

Analise just brewed her first batch of beer. She read a couple of books before her first brew and even visited the local home-brew shop. She felt prepared and satisfied as she laid out her ingredients and equipment on her kitchen table. She lives in a small five-story walk-up with a great view of the skyline over Lake Michigan.

Unfortunately, in the frosty winter months, Analise has no heating. (In fact, she wears sweats, an oversized comfy sweater, big furry slippers, and a beanie while unpacking her brewing supplies and pouring pre-milled grain into a mesh bag.) Analise spent hours lovingly mashing in on her stovetop and then bringing the wort to a boil. Cooling the wort to the right temperature happened especially fast and with ease. She had bought dehydrated yeast and decided to grow it up instead of pitching it dry to make sure the culture was viable and active. Then she pitched the starter that she'd grown up over three days. Even though it had taken longer than normal, Analise had seen initial signs of fermentation in her yeast starter and was sure everything would go smoothly. Now peering into the carboy, the wort just lies there lifeless and cold like yesterday's cup of coffee. After all her diligent work and patience, this is indeed a frustrating affair. All her time and effort ruined by the cold environment.

Meanwhile, Jordan had finally taken that class on fresh bread making and couldn't wait to try it at home. He always throws the best dinner parties, but this one would be different. With the addition of homemade bread, it would be his most memorable get-together yet. He invited his guests to come over

Friday night, ready to impress everyone with his newly found skills. Just the thought of the smell of hot bread coming out of the oven put a smile on his face.

On the day of the party, Jordan woke up extra early to make sure the dough would be ready for its first rise before the supermarket opened. (He planned to buy all the ingredients for tonight's dinner while the dough was rising.) The morning air was still brisk as he poured the flour into the yeast and water mixture—and then gently kneaded the dough. The water felt colder than normal, and Jordan wondered if he should have added a bit of hot water to balance out the temperature. He left the dough covered on his countertop under a cracked-open windowsill, facing the rising sun, while he went off to buy his groceries. It must have been a little over an hour when Jordan arrived back home, only to find the dough looking the same as when he left. The disappointment was overwhelming.

Both of these scenarios have and will happen when baking and brewing. Sometimes you do everything right, but your wort shows no signs of fermentation and your dough will sit there with no noticeable change. How can you really discern if yeast is doing its job? It's hard to know what to do in these scenarios. With practice and experience—and a couple of hints from this book—the process will not be as daunting.

When baking bread, **if the room temperature is too cold**—even though the yeast is alive and viable—there will be no signs of active fermentation. The yeast will lie dormant and feed off nutrients reserved for hibernation. In this case, **it's best to move the dough to a warmer spot**

in the house. Placing your bowl of rising dough into an insulated space, such as an oven that is off, is often your best choice. It will retain heat even though it's not actively heating. Within 10 minutes of moving your dough, it should start to rise. If you notice that your workspace is colder than usual, this problem can be prevented in the mix. By using half boiling water and half filtered water from the tap or refrigerator, Jordan can balance out the temperature and make sure it's comfortable for yeast to grow. The ideal dough temperature is 75 to 78°F (23.9 to 25.6°C).

When waiting on your home brew to start showing signs of fermentation, it can be very frustrating. Even if the brewing process thus far had gone perfectly for Analise, there could still be issues at this stage. Optimizing the yeast performance and assuring its peak health is the brewer's main job. Yeast will do its job if you do yours. Failing at this point in the brewing process can mean a lot of time and effort down the drain, literally. Many brewers have had to dump batches of beer because of subpar fermentation. **A cold room can be one of the main culprits in a stuck fermentation.** The initial wait can be 24 hours or even more before seeing or hearing the yeast in action. **Placing blankets over and around your carboy or fermentation vessel will help insulate your wort and give gentle warmth to kick-start a stuck fermentation. Aeration is another way to make your yeast happy and multiply again.** Proper aeration can make sluggish fermentation vigorous. To aerate your wort, gently tip the carboy to one side—not too far! You don't want anything to spill. Rock the carboy in circular motions for a few minutes and then stop, switching directions. Each time you rock your carboy, you'll see the liquid funnel downward, similar to the way a twister in motion appears. Repeat this for roughly 10 to 30 minutes, depending on how cold the environment is and how quickly the wort is responding. Soon, you'll see frothy bubbles on the top of your wort as the yeast is redistributed throughout.

STORAGE

Brewing cultures, or pitches, should be kept cold in an airtight container that has been sanitized. This is the opposite of bread making where you are encouraged to get your hands dirty and deep inside the dough. A brewer must take precautions that no foreign cultures or bacteria will infiltrate and ruin or change the desired culture for use. A brewer keeps yeast cold to prevent the yeast from being active in a nutrient-deficient environment. Warm active yeast, without the proper nutrient environment, will stress out and autolyze (programmed cell death). A brewer keeps the container airtight to prevent oxygen from oxidizing the yeast environment and allow the air to bring in contaminants. Think bacteria and mold that are all too happy to use cold, dormant yeast as a food source.

Before + During Fermentation

Once a brewer decides to use a culture pitch, he will remove the container from the fridge and allow the yeast to rise to the temperature of a cooled wort. The wort has had yeast nutrients—such as fatty acids, zinc, and free aminos—added to it in the boil kettle already. After cooling through a heat exchanger, oxygen gas dissolves into the wort, either via an oxygen stone or through aerating the wort for 10 to 30 minutes. The wort then settles to 64.4 to 69.8°F (18 to 21°C) for ales or 50 to 57.2°F (10 to 14°C) for a lager. At this point, the yeast culture should be pitched. (As always, be sure to use sanitizer on all open surfaces, as contaminants are able to hitch a ride from yeast container to fermentor.)

Once in fermentation, it's critical to keep *Saccharomyces* at a cool temperature. Using an airlock or blowoff tube will prevent oxygen ingress back into the fermentor, which would stifle fermentation and oxidize the wort. As fermentation progresses, it's important to free-rise the temperature of the beer to 75.2°F (24°C) for a diacetyl (slow increase in temperature) rest. This will allow the yeast to fully metabolize all of its by-products.

When bakers bring it home from the store, dry active yeast or instant dry rapid rise yeast should also be stored cold to make sure the yeast is not thrust into activity prematurely. Check the use-by date on the package (it typically reflects two years into the future from the packaging date). A baker can keep these yeast in the freezer or refrigerator in a sealed package or airtight container for three or four months. As long as outside contaminants don't get in and temperature is maintained, the yeast should stay latent yet ready to get to work. At room temperature or on a shelf in the supermarket, dry active yeast or instant dry rapid rise yeast will lose activity over time. When the package is opened and yeast is exposed to air, moisture, or heat, yeast will be susceptible to outside contaminants.

Finally, when it's time to use active dry yeast or instant rapid rise yeast, bring it to room temperature before using. Active dry yeast needs to be dissolved in warm water to wake it up from dormancy. Instant dry or rapid rise yeast can be added straight to the flour. Unlike sourdough, you won't be able to reuse these yeast in the next batch of dough. An old dough starter, however, is an excellent addition for flavor and texture—but not to leaven the bread.

After Fermentation

When you're ready to store the yeast, you must assure the condition of the yeast. Fermentation history will allow you to know how many generations the cultures have grown, what beers they fermented, and if the beers were healthy. The more beers a culture ferments, the more generations it undergoes. Generally speaking, you don't want to use more than 10 generations for a *Saccharomyces* yeast strain.

If a yeast culture has just fermented a high-alcohol beer, it may not be a good candidate for reuse since it's already been through a stressed fermentation environment and is likely to be sluggish and produce off-flavors. That's because alcohol concentrations of 10% or more can offset the osmolarity of the yeast environment, and the yeast will be challenged to maintain a homeostatic state. Another thing to consider is that with every pitch and repitch, the likelihood of bacterial contamination overtaking the culture increases.

Likewise, sourdough cultures should be kept in a cool environment. If a baker is not baking every day, they'll most likely store the starter in a closed container in the refrigerator. Unlike beer starters, it's not important to sanitize your storage container, but the container should be clean and free of dried starter or other contaminants that may ruin a dormant starter. A cold environment will help it to remain inactive in long periods between bakes. (Otherwise, a warm place and no feedings can stress a starter out, causing it to become sick or even die.)

Once you're ready to use the sourdough to bake with, take it out of the cold and feed it flour and water. The amount of flour and water depends on the desired hydration and volume of the final culture. At this point, the sourdough starter can be stored at room temperature indefinitely, with feedings every 12 to 24 hours, so long as the temperature is around 75.2°F (24°C).

CULTIVATED STRAINS

Variations in *Saccharomyces cerevisiae* strains are plentiful on the market. Each strain comes with its own special requirements and characteristics. It's important to know which strain you're working with so you can care for your particular yeast. And as its caretaker, you can domesticate it.

Bakers or brewers may start off with a strain and create a hospitable environment for their yeast. The temperature that the yeast is grown and stored in, as well as the actual place, city, or country that the fermentation is taking place, will have a great influence of which strain will survive. Even the microbes on the baker or brewer's hands can either domesticate, change, or harm the original strain of yeast.

Brettanomyces

Let's start with sourdough starters: Most include a lot of *Lactobacilli*—bacteria, not yeast. *Saccharomyces* usually finds its way into sourdough starters simply through the air (especially in bakeries) and from a person's skin. If you were to send a bakery's sourdough starter to the lab, you might also find *Saccharomyces exiguus,* a wild yeast found on plants, fruits, and grains. Although not as well known, it is commonly used in bread baking without the knowledge of the baker.

At Long Beach Beer Lab and its adjoining bakery in Southern California, the sourdough starter is made mostly of *Brettanomyces.* This yeast is thought to have been cultivated from the skins of grapes in its initial formation. In further analysis, there is a question whether the *Brettanomyces* came from the grapes themselves or if it was domesticated through being exposed to beer cultures at the brewery. This strain of *Brettanomyces* is unique in that it produces lactic acid, which gives the bread and beer fermented with it a nice tart flavor.

Saccharomyces cerevisiae

Saccharomyces cerevisiae is the strain most widely used in bread making. Baker's yeast is one of the oldest food microbial starters. There are patents on more than 150 inventions over 300-plus baker's yeast strains. Some of the first patents boasted an improved biomass yield, higher gassing power in dough, or a better survival rate. There have been improvements in baker's yeast strains to help them stand up to higher fat or sugar contents in dough, as well as helping them withstand being stored at cold to freezing temperatures. There are even patented baker's yeast strains that claim better aroma, anti-molding, and a higher nutrient content. Science has gone on to genetically engineer some yeast, but these strains haven't caught on in the baking industry and are mostly used in the pharmaceutical and biofuel industries.

Interestingly, baker's yeast is a species of *Saccharomyces cerevisiae* and is the same species as brewer's yeast. Although they are the same species, they're different strains. Still, some strains of brewer's yeast can also be used to bake bread. For example, Nottingham, an English style ale yeast strain, can be used in a similar way as a sourdough starter. This yeast imparts a sweet malty flavor, a beautiful rise, and slightly dense and soft crumb. Even though some brewer's yeast can be used in bread making, using baker's yeast in beer making can leave a beer under-attenuated and watery. The upshot? With so many brewer's yeast strains to choose from, leave the baker's yeast to the bakers.

Strains

Commercial laboratories carry a number of yeast cultures for each style of beer. There are strains for ale, lager, Belgian, and sour beer. Within these styles, there are a myriad of subcategories, each with their own unique strain. Ale yeast, for example, is a species of *Saccharomyces cerevisiae* and is a top fermenter. Lager yeast, a species of *Saccharomyces uvarum* or *Saccharomyces carlsbergensis,* is a bottom-fermenting strain.

The Beer Judge Certification Program (BJCP) has organized about 88 different styles of beer with the ability to use multiple yeast strains in each, leaving more than 200 yeast strains to choose from. Each style has specific guidelines set forth by the BJCP, with particular flavor profiles that must be met. In order to get the flavors just right, yeast will need to carry its job out flawlessly, while the brewer must nurture the yeast during this process. In American ales, yeast must remain as neutral as possible—by holding 64.4 to 68°F (10 to 20°C) during fermentation—in order for the other ingredients, like hops and malt, to shine. For Belgian ales and saisons, the yeast can ferment at temperatures of 75.2 to 80.6°F (24 to 27°C) to get the phenolics and esters so often associated with classic Belgian ales and rustic saisons.

In lagers, yeast have their own limitations. Certain styles of lager, whether it be pilsner, helles, or wheat, will have a different strain of yeast in order to execute a specific profile character. Pilsner yeast will ferment cold at 53.6 to 57.2°F (12 to 14°C) to give off a crisp, sulfury character. On the other side, hefeweizen wheat beers are fermented warmer and impart banana and clove. When this fails, some commercial breweries will sometimes include adjunct ingredients, such as spices, tinctures, or even extracts.

WILD + OUT OF THIN AIR

Yeast is everywhere: It lies in wait on grains and lives naturally in the air and on the surfaces of fruits. It's no wonder wild yeast is used in bread and beer to bring out unique flavors and rare fermentation qualities. It is the gift that keeps on giving because wild yeast can be nurtured and kept for years, all the while becoming more complex while gaining strength and viability.

Wild (or spontaneous) fermentation is some of the most complex and alluring fermentation to exist. It's sought after by beer and bread enthusiasts everywhere and is dictated by the creator as much as by time and place—some might call it terroir. There is no better way to describe terroir in bread and beer than to delve into the microflora of a place to determine nuances and flavor. After all, yeast carry ester and phenolic flavor profiles deep in their genetic code, phenotypic expressions that depend on wherever they happen to be on Earth.

In beer, spontaneous inoculation of yeast from wind and air into a brewer's coolship (an open-top vessel in which fermentation starts in the open air without pitching yeast or a cover to protect the beer from the elements) is more art than science. Making sure the environment is correct to begin a fruitful fermentation requires an inviting wort. It means that climate, time, and place requirements are all met in order for a successful ferment. Usually cold weather at night in an area where microbiology thrives is key to a productive outcome. Consider the lush hills full of fruit trees in Belgium: It's no wonder these fermentations have existed in Belgian brewing since the beginning.

Keys to Success

A successful wild yeast ferment depends on some key factors. Most importantly, the temperature has to be 64.4 to 68°F (18 to 20°C). The composition of the wort with a huge amount of amino acids and dextrinous material for microbiology to feed off is equally key. This is why a turbid mash is encouraged. A turbid mash leaves unconverted starches and free aminos left in the wort, by way of high temperatures, for microbes to flourish in the coolship and lets wild yeast grow faster before negative bacterial growth can happen. And by bacterial growth, consider *Enterobacteriaceae* infection of wort, which can lead to undesirable outcomes and undrinkable beer. Such infections usually occur at high temperatures in the warmer months. This is the reason it is best to use the coldest time of the year, so *Saccharomyces* can take a lead role in the initial fermentation.

In order to make a sourdough starter, one must consider the same requirements. If you want to make a sourdough starter at home from scratch, it's best to use high-protein flours from rye or whole-wheat grains. Mix these grains with an equal amount of filtered water in a jar. If you let this mixture sit, you should see fermentation within a day or up to a week. To quicken the process and to impart deeper and more unique flavors and yeast strains, use fruit laden with natural yeast to encourage appropriate inoculation. Place the fruit around the jar with the lid of the jar cracked to allow for migration of yeast from fruit to the starting dough in the jar. Again, doing this in the colder months will help discourage *Enterobacteriaceae* growth, which otherwise makes a starter sick and seem thin and lifeless with a strange cheeselike smell. A healthy starter will smell sweet with fruity esters filling the nostrils. A great indicator of a successful wild capture is vigorous fermentation with rupturing carbon dioxide and overwhelming activity. Meanwhile, bacterial fermentation smells off-putting, like sulfur, rotten eggs, or rotting fruit.

A Unique Culture

If everything works out correctly, you're left with a unique spontaneous starter. This is how you can begin to build a true house culture with one-of-a-kind flavors. As time passes, the culture will express more or less, depending on the ups and downs of the seasons, giving variability and an art to the science of microbiology.

Later in this book, you'll find a few wild yeast–focused recipes as well as projects to give you firsthand experience working with these mysterious strains. In Chapter 4, you'll make a sourdough gose to demonstrate using a wild bread yeast to make a classic beer style. In Chapter 6, you'll learn how to turn your bread yeast into a beer starter with the help of a wild capture from fruit. You'll also experiment with an aged sour. This will show you how to use wild yeast in long-term beer fermentation.

FERMENTATION GEAR

In the following chapters, you'll take all of this know-how and use it to make delicious bread and beer. While it's excellent to read about beer and bread making, little will be learned or retained without putting it all into practice. You may already have a well-stocked kitchen or even own some of the equipment listed on pages 54 and 55. There are also many fancy gadgets—including a sous vide wand or proofing chamber—that you can purchase to make bread and beer, but these are not necessary unless you're looking to take your projects to the next level. The following are the basics needed to make a successful batch of beer and a fresh loaf of bread. Other than these items, simply bring a curious mind, a strong work ethic, patience, and of course love for what you're doing and are about to create.

Beer-making Equipment

Hydrometer: A device used to measure the density of wort in order to determine the gravity and the alcohol content of the beer.

Thermometer: Used to determine temperature of mash, boil, and cooled wort in the fermentation bucket.

Large Pot: For boiling wort, best to acquire a pot twice the volume of the wort you are boiling.

Sanitizer: Some brands such as Iodine or Star San are used to sanitize all surfaces to avoid contamination.

Bucket: A container to hold wort for fermentation. Best to use a 5-gallon bucket with a spigot, graduation markings, and a hole in the lid to place blowoff tube or airlock.

Airlock: A device that lets carbon dioxide escape the bucket but doesn't allow oxygen out of the bucket. An alternative would be a blowoff tube that extends from the lid of the bucket into a jar of water. It serves the same purpose as the designed airlock.

Racking Cane: An auto siphon tool to transfer beer from the one container to another. The purpose of a racking cane is to decrease oxidation and contamination during transfer.

Mesh Bag: For steeping grain in the boil kettle. Make sure this bag is temperature resistant.

Erlenmeyer Flask: A container to grow a yeast starter.

Scale: Preferably digital to measure the weight of hops and malt.

Bread-making Equipment

Mixing Bowl or Tub: A rather deep, large vessel used for weighing ingredients into and mixing the dough.

Bench Knife or Dough Scraper: A straight-edge metal rectangle with a handle along one side. It is primarily used for scraping dough from a work surface. It is also used to cut dough into portioned pieces. A bench knife will come in handy for many other things as well.

Flexible Dough Scraper: A flexible plastic rectangle used as a flat spatula to scrape out a bowl or clean work surfaces.

Digital Thermometer: An instrument for measuring both water and dough temperature.

Digital Scale, Measuring Cups, Spoons: To measure the weight or volume of the ingredients.

Proofing Basket or Loaf Pan: A vessel used to provide structure for shaped loaves of bread during proofing. It is usually used for doughs that are too soft or wet for holding their shape.

RECIPES

CHAPTER 4

BEER

Yeast in action is a phenomenal and awe-inspiring sight. The billowing pops of healthy fermentation are like music to the ears. Home brewing is a wonderful hobby, but the only way to really delve into the art of fermentation is by application. So enough studying and theorizing: It's time to get fired up about beer making! In this chapter, you will find a practical guide and recipes that will take your home-brewing skills to the next level.

BREWER'S TO-DO LIST

Home brewing on a small scale can be fun and easy enough to control and clean up. You may have already made a batch of beer either with friends or on your own, but here's a quick reminder of the steps.

1. Gather all equipment and weigh out ingredients.

2. Pour grain into a fine-knit brew bag and tie it off. (For all grain recipes, double-check your malt is milled or mill it yourself.)

3. Fill a pot with water and bring it to 154°F (67°C). Add full brew bag to the pot of water and let steep for 60 minutes.

4. Remove brew bag from pot and bring remaining liquid to a boil again.

5. Pour hops into a fine-knit brew bag and add to boiling water for 60 minutes.

6. Remove hops and add optional yeast nutrient.

7. Nestle pot into a prepared ice bath to cool the wort according to the recipe. Put the cooled wort into a fermentation vessel to cool further.

8. Aerate or shake up the fermentation vessel.

9. Pitch dehydrated or liquid yeast starter.

10. Place in a temperature-controlled area.

11. Wait until fermentation is complete.

12. Bottle up and enjoy!

Pitching Precision

In the beginning, you might have assumed that the more yeast you add, the better the fermentation. But there are consequences. Having too much yeast may cause fermentation to speed up and go too quickly. Instead, it's better to pitch the correct amount of yeast, let it do its job, and ferment for the proper time. If yeast is overpitched, flavor compounds and mouthfeel can seem like they're missing something, and the beer will be watery and lackluster. That's because yeast will skip their growth or lag phases altogether. If there is too little yeast pitched, the beer may have a stuck fermentation or act sluggish with intermediate fermentation. The flavor compounds such as ethyl acetate, diacetyl, or isoamyl acetate will be noticeable when you take a sip, the beer sweet and containing undesirable something's-not-right flavors.

How to Aerate

Aerating the wort after pitching the yeast is a small but crucial step. It gets oxygen to the newly producing yeast for sterol compounds used to build yeast cell walls. This in turn will make the yeast stronger, so the beer will look, taste, and smell outstanding.

1. Fill the fermentation container with fresh cooled wort.

2. Cap the container tightly so no wort spills.

3. Rock the container on its edge for 15 to 30 minutes until sufficiently aerated.

4. Pitch yeast into a freshly aerated wort and place an airlock cap on the container ready for fermentation.

Cleanliness and sanitation are the hallmarks of great brewing. Pre-fermented wort or beer is a digestible and nutritious food source— especially for bacteria, who love the malted barley sugars and free amino acids. That said, there are key steps to avoid creating a habitat for bacteria. After the boil is complete, any surface the beer touches must be sanitized with iodine or commercial-grade sanitizer. The fermentation bucket or carboy should be thoroughly rinsed with sanitizer for at least 1 minute. Any hoses used during transfer are also to be soaked in a sanitizer solution, as well as the airlock and container bung. While you're at it, spray the opening yeast container or yeast packet. Any other materials added to the beer wort should be boiled prior to its addition.

Yeast's To-Do List

Yeast are introduced to aerated beer wort after the boil has been cooled down to the proper fermentation temperature. Before it's added, dehydrated packet yeast must be rehydrated in pasteurized clean water that's also been cooled to fermentation temperatures.

Adding dry yeast directly to the pre-fermented wort is not advised. The different sugar concentrations in the wort and the dehydrated yeast cell will cause the cell to go into sugar shock. That is why pure water is suggested to rehydrate yeast. When using wet yeast, the temperature must be brought up to the same fermentation temperature being used.

Once the yeast is pitched into the wort, it begins to feed on the most readily available sugar sources, primarily glucose and dextrose. Once the yeast have sufficient energy, they'll start to reproduce in a 12- to 48-hour period known as the lag phase, in which oxygen and free amino acids are used to make sterols and protein for future yeast. There will be seemingly no activity in the fermentor or airlock, but—have faith!—the yeast are hard at work.

Things get action-packed from here: All of a sudden, activity will start, and the swirling mixtures of wort and protein in the fermentation bucket or carboy can be seen vividly. Multitudes of yeast will be rushing to metabolize any sugar source they can find, working from the simplest to the more complex as fermentation progresses: glucose to dextrose to maltose to maltotriose. They will stop at the long chain dextrins that they can't metabolize. Yeast will use their carbon dioxide by-product almost like mini jetpacks to lift themselves higher and higher into the unfermented wort toward a larger source of unfermented sugars.

Once all sugar sources are consumed, the yeast aggregate and flocculate out of suspension. After active fermentation has died, yeast cells clump together, and the carbon dioxide production decreases. Gravity does what it does and causes the yeast to fall to the bottom of the fermentor. The brewer steps in here and removes the beer for packaging, leaving behind the yeast at the bottom of the fermentor to be stored and reused later.

Throughout packaging, during the transfer of beer to bottles, some yeast will migrate along. You could add a simple priming sugar to the bottle to encourage a mini refermentation in the bottle—known as bottle conditioning. Usually this sugar will be some form of glucose, sucrose, or dextrose. Yeast referment these simple sugars to alcohol and carbon dioxide, adding that distinct fizz that makes beer so refreshing for the drinker.

THE CRABTREE EFFECT

Yeast are facultative anaerobes, which means they can produce energy with or without oxygen. As discussed, when a brewer seals a carboy with an airlock or blowoff, oxygen is extremely limited and yeast will undergo anaerobic respiration to produce alcohol and carbon dioxide, and suddenly Krebs Cycle—which you might remember from high school bio class and is also known as the TCA cycle—becomes impossible, slowing energy production.

If oxygen is present in fermenting yeast, glycolysis pyruvate is thrust into the mitochondria and the Krebs Cycle will take place through a process known as oxidative phosphorylation, or respiration. In the presence of oxygen, yeast make more ATP, or energy, and carbon dioxide plus water as a result.

The Crabtree Effect takes place when malted sugar sources are high in the presence of oxygen, and yeast will still prefer to produce alcohol and carbon dioxide even though less energy is made. Yeast can turn on and off respiration as they see fit, and in the presence of simple sugars, they tend to produce alcohol. It's thought this is owing to the antiseptic properties of alcohol and its ability to allow yeast to thrive by sterilizing its environment from pesky bacteria.

PERFORMANCE REVIEW

There are many ways to test yeast performance throughout fermentation. The easiest way to check on yeast health is looking through the glass carboy to see if there is any activity in the ferment.

Ultimately, though, the most scientific method is to check attenuation by using a hydrometer. A hydrometer measures the density of a liquid. The more sugars in the wort or beer, the higher the gravity. Water has a gravity of 1 SG, or specific gravity. As yeast ferment beer, the gravity falls closer and closer to 1 SG.

If a brewer is noticing a sluggish ferment, there are several things they can do to salvage the batch. First, you could shake the fermentor to rouse the yeast back into suspension—or simultaneously reoxygenate the beer and add heat. If that doesn't work, it's possible to pitch another batch of yeast to see if the second batch can get the job done.

If yeast overachieved and the beer finishes super dry with no residual body or mouthfeel, it is possible to add *lactose* or *maltodextrin* to the beer to regain the perception of a fuller and meatier body. Additionally, in future brews, the brewer can rebrew the recipe with a higher mash temperature to leave long chain dextrins unmodified.

TYPES + PROFILES

The two most common types of brewing yeast are ale and lager. There is also a third type that's becoming more common these days—our old friend *Brettanomyces*, a wild yeast strain notorious for producing wild ales. With these three broad categories come unique flavor profiles and fermentation qualities. Each has a myriad of specific and unique substrains that lend that last touch of flavor to a beer.

Brettanomyces, for example, is a top-fermenting yeast that loves to produce wild fermentation flavors, such as tropical fruit, barnyard hay, and horse blanket. It also favors higher fermentation temperatures, around 68 to 78.8°F (20 to 27°C) and is great to co-ferment in Belgian saison ales.

Ales, *Saccharomyces cerevisiae*, are top-fermenting yeast tending to like a warmer fermentation temperature somewhere between 64.4 and 68°F (18 and 24°C). Owing to the higher temperatures, it's common to see ales ferment faster and portray a bouquet of fruity or pepper flavors. The foamy krausen hovering on top of an ale fermentation can be used to inoculate another batch of ale to keep fermentations ongoing and continuous.

Lagers, *Saccharomyces pastorianus*, are bottom-fermenting yeast preferring colder temperature. Lagers most commonly ferment at 50 to 60.8°F (10 to 16°C). They take about three times as long to complete fermentation. It's common practice to lager— or store cold—the finished beer for an additional amount of time to let the yeast clean up the beer from fermentation flavor by-products. The result is a crisp and refreshing beer with little fermentation flavor and a focus on malt grains and noble hops.

Dry Yeast

It's best to use dry yeast in common brewing styles, as the strains are limited. Brewers use dry yeast in a pinch owing to their ease in storage and transport. The ability to pitch larger rates of cells is easier in dry yeast and can be used to supplement liquid yeast.

Liquid Yeast

Liquid yeast have increased strain variability, and the yeast cells themselves tend to be more viable. With appropriate planning, liquid yeast can be ordered and stored for a short period of time before use. Factor in lower pitching rates because cell viability is higher. Since strain variability is vast in liquid yeast, a brewer can make extremely specific beer styles.

YEAST STYLES REFERENCE GUIDE

Yeast	Beer Style	Flavors
California Ale Yeast	IPA	Neutral flavors and clean alcohol production
English Ale Yeast	Extra Special Bitter	Stone fruit, banana, clove
Belgian Ale Yeast	Witbier	Pepper, clove, banana, bubblegum, stone fruit
German Lager Yeast	Helles Lager	Sulfur, grain, apple
Czech Pilsner Yeast	Bohemian Pilsner	Sulfur, pepper, grain

BREWER'S RECIPES

The following recipes are designed to highlight different aspects of yeast fermentation. Each beer will be wholly unique—because of the yeast, its strain, and how the brewer can manipulate it for desired flavors, colors, carbonation, and more. These recipes were designed for a brew-in-a-bag method. So instead of using many different pots and spending money on expensive equipment, you only need one large pot and a large porous bag similar to a paint-straining bag.

Most yeast can be found commercially online or locally. The type of yeast will dictate the outcome of flavors in the brew. Be sure to treat the yeast the way the recipe intends. Temperature control and modulation are of the utmost importance. So are measurements: By all means, please read a recipe thoroughly before starting it, and weigh everything out using a digital scale. Each recipe begins with a special Yeast at Work tutorial in yeast management, so take in all the yeast has to offer and enjoy.

SCALING DOWN

Please note the following recipes are for 2.5-gallon batches. It's important to size your equipment based on the batch size, so for 2.5 gallons of beer, a brewer needs about two times the amount of water. Sizing the pot should be adequate to boil 5 gallons of water. Once you have a good-sized pot, be sure to double-check that it can hold the grain bag and all additional equipment accordingly.

Scaling a brewing recipe isn't exactly linear: Thermodynamics and utilization vary on physical sizes of equipment and the mass of the grain bill. For the sake of these recipes, the focus on yeast profiles and lessons on a linear scale will suffice. For a 1-gallon recipe, you can divide the recipe in half to get an accurate outcome. If more beer is your desire, doubling the recipe will bring the batch up to 5 gallons—the typical home-brew recipe size.

YEAST AT WORK:
SLOW AND COLD FERMENTATION

With appropriate temperature control in long, cold ferments, one can make an excellent, clean, and crisp lager. Fermentation flavors are a by-product of hotter and faster temperatures, so to control yeast flavor and focus on malt or hops, look to colder fermentation temperatures. The fermentation process goes something like this:

1. Put carboy in fridge for 1 day.

2. Transfer carboy to keg bucket with ice for 3 days, replenishing ice every day.

3. Add ice to keg bucket more infrequently for 3 weeks.

4. After 3 weeks, place carboy back in the fridge to lager for 3 weeks.

Additionally, yeast strains will dictate flavor profiles, so be sure to pick the right yeast for the job. German lager yeast are great for helles lagers, which are clean and crisp with a focus on malt and hops. A neutral ale yeast, like a California ale, gives off little fermentation flavors and can do the trick as well but is more suited to higher temperatures.

continued

CRISP HELLES LAGER

Makes 2.5 gallons

This lager is crisp, light, and clear with an amazing mouthfeel and medium body. It is a perfect accompaniment to a backyard BBQ. Saccharomyces pastorianus is the yeast of choice with variations like Fermentis, SafAle, SafLager, German Lager Yeast, or W34/70. This yeast variant is a weihenstephaner cultivar that delivers a crisp and grainy malt character to a light and refreshing beer.

When working with lagers, it is very important to use temperature control. A lager is classically fermented at cooler temperatures. While other styles of beer will do best at an ambient temperature that is readily available in your home, lagers must be fermented in a controlled environment. To do this with no off-flavors, you must have some way of controlling the fermentation temperature. If you do not have a dedicated fermentation chamber, a small refrigerator with a dial to turn the temperature up or down may be used.

Equipment	Ingredients
Large pot	Carbon-filtered water
Brew bag	4 lb American pilsner malt
Hops bag	0.4 lb American white wheat malt
Carboy	0.60 oz Hallertau hops (3.8% alpha acid)
Keg bucket	¼ tsp yeast nutrient
Temperature-controlled chamber (or small fridge)	Ice
	6 grams Bavarian lager yeast

1. In a large pot, bring 5 gallons of water to 154°F (67°C).

2. Place malts in a brew bag and add the bag to the pot of water to steep for 60 minutes.

3. Remove brew bag and squeeze excess liquid from bag into the pot. Bring the wort to a rolling boil for 30 minutes.

4. Place hops in a hops bag and add bag to the boiling wort to steep for 60 minutes.

5. Remove the hops bag and add yeast nutrient. Place the large pot into an ice bath, using the keg bucket, to cool to 64.5°F (18°C).

6. Place the cooled wort into the carboy and into the fridge to bring it to 53.5°F (12°C). Shake the carboy to aerate the wort.

7. Place the carboy into the keg bucket ice bath and pitch the yeast. Continually add ice to the keg bucket for 3 days of fermentation.

8. While leaving the carboy in the keg bucket, allow the fermentation to free-rise to 64.4°F (18°C).

continued

9. After active fermentation is done and bubbling in the airlock has stopped, add ice back to the keg bucket to make an ice bath, and bring temperature down to 39.2°F (4°C). Then place carboy into the refrigerator for 3 weeks.

10. Package or bottle up, and enjoy!

Best Practices: Stuck ferments are common in lighter lagers. Be sure to use extra aeration and yeast nutrients. In order to attenuate this lager to completion, after the first three days, be sure to allow the fermentation temperature to free-rise to 64.4°F (18°C).

YEAST AT WORK:
HOT AND FAST FERMENTATION

The lesson here is to show how higher temperatures in ale yeast strains show off typical Belgian flavor profiles—bubblegum, banana, pepper, and clove are phenols and esters given off in a hot and fast fermentation. Belgian yeast are known to enjoy hotter fermentations and tend to give off the best balance of these flavors. To be clear, any ale yeast will work at hotter temperatures, but Belgian yeast strains are best suited to give those classic flavor profiles that are associated with the style.

The fermentation looks like this:

1. Allow fermentation carboy to rise to room temperature for 1 day.

2. Use a small desk heater to bring the carboy temperature to 80°F (27°C) over 3 days.

3. Allow carboy to cool to room temperature over 1 day, and then place it in the fridge.

continued

RUSTIC WIT

Makes 2.5 gallons

This is a traditional Belgian witbier using stock ale instead of orange peel and coriander to achieve those classic Belgian flavors. This recipe calls for Hoegaarden witbier yeast or WLP400 to allow for the classic bubblegum and clove characteristics everyone is familiar with. To get more pepper and citrus flavors as well as a touch of complexity, the beer is topped off with store-bought sour ale. The grain bill supports this beer with a pillowy and doughy mouthfeel. After a sip, you'll agree that this is a super-drinkable, crisp wheat beer bursting with flavor.

Equipment

Large pot

Brew bag

Hops bag

Carboy

Keg bucket

Temperature-controlled chamber (or small fridge)

Ingredients

Carbon-filtered water

2.5 lb American pilsner malt

2.5 lb American white wheat

0.65 oz of saaz hops (3.8% alpha acid)

¼ tsp yeast nutrient

Ice

6 grams Belgian Hoegaarden witbier ale yeast

12 oz store-bought sour ale

1. In a large pot, bring 5 gallons of water to 147°F (64°C).

2. Place malts in a brew bag and add the bag to the pot of water to steep for 60 minutes.

3. Remove brew bag and squeeze excess liquid from bag into the pot. Bring the wort to a rolling boil for 30 minutes.

4. Place hops in a hops bag and add bag to the boiling wort to steep for 60 minutes.

5. Remove the hops bag and add yeast nutrient. Place the large pot into an ice bath, using the keg bucket, to cool to 64.5°F (18°C).

6. Place the cooled wort into the carboy and into the fridge to bring it to 39.2°F (4°C). Shake the carboy to aerate the wort.

continued

Best Practices: Ferment this beer warm starting at 68°F (20°C). Next, let it free-rise to 78.8°F (26°C). This will allow the yeast to express its classic Belgian note while also making sure the beer ends up crisp and dry. This refreshing ale's use of stock or store-bought sour ale will enhance the complexity of the beer with notes of citrus and pepper.

7. Place the carboy into the keg bucket ice bath and pitch the yeast. Continually add ice to the keg bucket for 3 days of fermentation.

8. Remove the carboy from the cold water and allow the ferment to free-rise to 80.6°F (27°C).

9. After active fermentation is done and bubbling in the airlock has stopped, place the carboy in a 39.2°F (4°C) refrigerator for 2 days.

10. Add the store-bought sour ale and mix thoroughly.

11. Package or bottle up, and enjoy!

YEAST AT WORK:
BREAD-MEETS-BEER FERMENTATION

A sourdough starter can work well both in baking and brewing. Yes, it's an advanced application in brewing with an experimental edge. But it's a fun one that shows how to use mixed fermentation qualities of a wild yeast starter laden with bacteria to produce acid quickly at extremely high temperatures. To prop up the sourdough starter for this recipe, follow these directions (or buy a lactic acid pitch from an online yeast bank):

1. Mix 10 grams high-protein flour with 10 grams filtered water.

2. Add 6 grams seed sourdough starter.

3. Let this ripen over 24 hours, and then pitch it into the carboy.

4. Bung the carboy with the airlock.

5. Place the carboy into a keg bucket.

6. Set a sous vide wand to 104°F (40°C).

7. Let it sit for 48 hours. You should be able to taste a distinct acidity in the wort.

continued

THAT'S HOW IT GOSE

Makes 2.5 gallons

A sourdough gose is an experimental style aiming for a traditional one. The recipe uses new techniques to push the envelope on yeast fermentation. Your next-level equipment list includes a sous vide wand to regulate the wort temperature to 104°F (40°C). The wort will be fermented with a wild capture sourdough starter before getting boiled again and finished with an American ale yeast.

Equipment

Large pot

Brew bag

Hop bag

Carboy

Keg bucket

Submersible heating source (sous vide wand or aquarium heater)

Temperature-controlled chamber (or small fridge)

Ingredients

Carbon-filtered water

2.5 lb American pilsner malt

2.5 lb American white wheat malt

10 grams sea salt

20 grams sourdough starter (see Yeast at Work: Bread-Meets-Beer Fermentation, page 75)

0.65 oz of saaz hops (3.8% alpha acid)

6 grams American ale yeast

Ice

¼ tsp yeast nutrient

1. In a large pot, bring 5 gallons of water to 147°F (65°C).

2. Place malts in a brew bag and add the bag to the pot of water to steep for 60 minutes at 152.6°F (67°C).

3. Remove brew bag and squeeze excess liquid from bag into the pot. Bring the wort to a rolling boil for 30 minutes. Then let cool to 104°F (40°C).

4. Place the pot into a large water bath; place a sous vide tool into the water and set the bath to 104°F (40°C).

5. Pre-acidify the wort to 4.5 pH. Pitch sourdough starter to the pot and cover. Let wort ferment for 48 hours.

6. Bring pot to a boil. Place hops in a hops bag and add bag to the boiling wort to steep for 60 minutes.

continued

Best Practices: One effective way to keep a stable 104°F (40°C) is by placing a home kitchen sous vide device into a large water bath.

7. Remove the hops bag and add the yeast nutrient. Place the large pot into an ice bath, using the keg bucket, to cool to 64.5°F (18°C).

8. Place the cooled wort into the carboy and shake to aerate the wort. Place the carboy in the keg bucket full of cold water. Pitch the yeast and let ferment for 3 days.

9. Remove the fermentation bucket from the cold water and allow the ferment to free-rise to 80.6°F (27°C).

10. After active fermentation is done and bubbling in the airlock has stopped, place the bucket in 39.2°F (4°C) refrigerator for 2 days.

11. Package or bottle up, and enjoy!

YEAST AT WORK:
FERMENTATION WITH LIMITED OXYGEN

Sour ale is the champagne of brewing. The yeast techniques here are subtle and in the longterm produce the most pronounced results. The focus here is to limit the amount of oxygen to the beer over time to protect it from staling and from *Brettanomyces* turning alcohol into acetic acid in the presence of oxygen.

Working with yeast is a practice in patience, endurance, and diligence. There's the required attention to cleanliness, art of temperature and oxygen control, and, of course, long aging process. The brewer's rewards, though, are fascinating flavors and fermentation characteristics. Here's how to do it:

1. Top off finished beer with new wort to decrease headspace and oxygen exposure.

2. Put in a cool dark place in your house, and secure the bung to decrease oxygen exposure.

3. Top up airlock so it doesn't dry out, and forget about the carboy for a year

continued

FARMER'S BLEND

Makes 2.5 gallons

A farmhouse wild ale is an exceptional ale that tests a brewer's patience in long fermentation with alternative yeast such as Brettanomyces or Wickerhamomyces. This American wild sour will be tart and at the same time complex with notes of sherry, stone fruit, and malty grain.

Equipment

Large pot

Brew bag

Hops bag

Carboy

Keg bucket

Temperature-controlled chamber (or small fridge)

Ingredients

Carbon-filtered water

2.5 lb American pilsner malt

1 lb American white wheat

1 lb rye malt

1 lb oats

0.35 oz aged Magnum hops (12% alpha acid)

¼ tsp yeast nutrient

Ice

6 grams mixed fermentation blend (WLP655 and Bootleg Biology Sour Solera Blend)

1. In a large pot, bring 5 gallons of water to 147°F (65°C).

2. Place malts in a brew bag and add the bag to the pot of water to steep for 60 minutes at 152.6°F (67°C). Remove brew bag and squeeze excess liquid from bag into the pot.

3. Bring pot to a boil. Place hops in a hop bag and add bag to the boiling wort to steep for 60 minutes.

4. Remove the hop bag and add the yeast nutrient. Place the large pot into an ice bath, using the keg bucket, to cool to 64.5°F (18°C).

5. Shake the fermentation bucket to aerate the wort. Then put the fermentation vessel back into the keg bucket full of cold water. Pitch the yeast and let ferment for 3 days.

continued

Best Practices: When souring for long periods of time it is important to minimize oxygen exposure to the beer. *Brettanomyces* and bacteria can use oxygen to convert ethanol to acetic acid. Make sure the fermentation bucket or carboy is topped up with beer as much as can be. Limit the amount of times the bucket or carboy is open to the air: That means don't constantly check your beer. Be patient, forget about it, and it will in turn reward you.

6. Remove fermentation vessel from the cold water and allow the ferment to free-rise to 80.6°F (27°C).

7. After active fermentation is done and bubbling in the airlock has stopped, place the bucket in a temperature-stable location—around 66.2°F (19°C). Fill fermentation vessel to the top, leaving very little headspace for oxygen. Be sure there are no oxygen leaks. Let age up to 1 year.

8. After a year, cold-crash the fermentation bucket at 39.2°F (4°C) for 2 days.

9. Package or bottle up, and enjoy!

RECIPES

CHAPTER 5

BREAD

Once you've baked your first loaf, it's tough to go back to the packaged supermarket variety. This chapter focuses on practical information and ways to make fresh bread a normal occurrence in your life. We could philosophize baking and bread yeast fermentation, but until you have actually put your hands into the dough, you'll never know the true joy of it. So get ready! The time has come to delve into the art and science of baker's yeast fermentation and bread making.

BAKER'S TO-DO LIST

Every recipe is different, and steps may vary. But here are the basic steps of bread making.

1. Weigh out all the ingredients.

2. Mix room-temperature water—68 to 77°F (20 to 25°C)—with yeast, pre-ferment, or culture.

3. Add any additions such as nuts, fruits, or herbs for even distribution.

4. Add and mix flour until it forms a dough ball.

5. Knead dough to incorporate oxygen and create carbon dioxide.

6. Leave dough to rise (for how long depends on the amount and type of yeast used).

7. Fold dough between risings.

8. Turn dough out onto a lightly floured work surface and divide.

9. Pre-shape dough and leave to rest, usually for about 30 minutes or until the dough has relaxed.

10. Reshape dough and let final rise free-form or in a basket or pan.

11. Bake until dough is golden brown and ready to eat.

YEAST'S TO-DO LIST

Baker's yeast lie dormant in their package or in a jar in the refrigerator, waiting for the moment they'll be awakened for bread making. The minute the yeast culture is exposed to water, especially if the water is warmer than where it was stored, the yeast will activate. When high-protein flour, diastatic malt, or sugar is added to the yeast and water mixture, the cells begin to exit dormancy and metabolize the sugars.

The water hydrates the flour, forming gluten strands. Kneading then adds heat, and gluten builds up while the yeast produce alcohol and carbon dioxide, trapping the gas for a voluminous rise. The highly elastic gluten strands are then stretched and left to relax, increasing extensibility in the dough and slowly building the gluten network, responsible for the crumb and texture of a loaf of bread.

PERFORMANCE REVIEW

Creating a hospitable environment for yeast has been the focus so far, but how do you really know if yeast is doing its job once a dough has formed? There are many simple checks to ensure that yeast fermentation is happening—and they start with your senses.

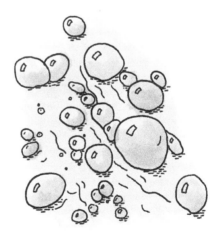

Looking for bubbles—or air pockets—on the surface of a rising dough is the most common and easiest of the checks. A dough will also increase in volume and be light to the touch. It should smell and even taste somewhat sweet, like ripe fruit.

If yeast doesn't seem to be in active fermentation, there could be a number of issues. It may be that the environment is too cold. In

SALT SCIENCE

Salt can assist the baker in many ways. Depending on how much salt is added, it can slow down or quicken the process of fermentation. The baker can then balance the pace of their dough fermentation. If no salt is added to the dough, fermentation will happen way too quickly.

Salt is hygroscopic, which means it attracts water. When salt is added to a dough, yeast release water through their cell walls. Yeast require a good deal of hydration to reproduce, so in the presence of salt, yeast will slow their fermentation. Too much salt and fermentation will lag to the point the bread will be left flat and lifeless. This is why salt is generally added to a recipe last to give the yeast, water, and flour time to interact.

this case, moving the dough to a warmer place should do the trick. It could be that the yeast is no longer viable. That is a tougher situation and can be solved by adding more yeast. Resolution of these issues will only come through experimentation and experience. Looking, touching, smelling, and even tasting your dough will tell you all you need to know.

TYPES AND PROFILES

Using different cultures can impart all kinds of flavors to your bread recipe. Yeast cultures come in many different forms, from fresh compressed cake yeast to dry yeast to doughy sourdough starters and pre-ferments. The culture you end up using will determine fermentation speed as well as the complexity of taste and overall success of your final bread. Some doughs are meant for a slow fermentation that comes with using sourdough starter. Others will turn out best using active dry or instant rapid rise yeast. Then there are other recipes that use a mixture of fresh yeast and a pre-ferment—perhaps even sourdough with a small amount of instant rapid rise yeast to save the baker time and support fermentation. On page 48 you'll find a few examples of these cultures, what they are, and how to use them.

Active Dry vs. Instant Rapid Rise

Active dry yeast is yeast that's been dried and therefore thrust into dormancy. It's granular and looks and feels like cornmeal. Before you incorporate it into a dough, you dissolve it in water.

Instant rapid rise yeast has an increased carbon dioxide production and is dried at a gentler temperature than active dry yeast. Most yeast cells can survive this drying process and in turn will be more viable. It's also finer in its consistency and can be added directly to the flour in a bread recipe. Many times, these yeast will be used interchangeably, but because instant rapid rise yeast will lead to a more vigorous fermentation, caution should be taken.

Types of Pre-ferments

There are many different kinds of pre-ferments. Each one has its own purpose and use. Following is a short description of the pre-ferments that are most commonly used. Each one has a particular benefit that will work well in different types of breads.

Old Dough: Also known as *pâte fermentée*, old fermented dough is saved and then added to a recipe to increase the overall quality of the dough. This dough can be made and fermented for two to three hours to use in a recipe, or it could be dough saved from a previous mix, as long as it's stored in the refrigerator at 35 to 40°F (1.6 to 4.4°C) for no more than 48 hours. For a baker who doesn't bake every day, it can be frozen for up to a week. (Old dough has a limited life expectancy and will lose vigor if kept around too long.) This technique was developed to add flavor and acidification to doughs that lack complexity. It's the only pre-ferment with salt in it, which should be taken into consideration when incorporating salt into your final mix. Pre-fermented dough is very versatile and can be used in croissants, Danish, baguettes, and rye breads.

Poolish: With a loose, liquidlike consistency, poolish is made with an equal amount of flour and water plus a small amount of yeast. Poolish ferments at room temperature for 12 to 24 hours. It was developed to give a deeper flavor to doughs without overt acidity and is known for increasing extensibility in dough, which makes shaping easier as well as increases volume. Poolish is mostly used in baguettes but has a place in other breads and some pastries.

Biga: Used for all Italian pre-ferments, a classic biga is thicker and stiffer than a traditional poolish. Unlike other pre-ferments, a biga has a constant fermentation temperature and time. At 50% hydration, the flour and water are mixed with a small amount of yeast, then held at 60°F (15.5°C) for 18 hours. The stiff consistency and cooler fermentation temperature provide a lot of strength to the dough. Take caution to not add too much biga to a recipe, which could limit extensibility, and favor it in brioche or stollen recipes, which require a stronger dough for proper texture and support. Biga can also be used in higher-hydration doughs to give them the volume they need.

Sponge: The sponge method is similar to the poolish process. A small amount of yeast is added to aid in a quick fermentation. It is relatively stiffer than a poolish and should only be used when it reaches full maturation (bubbles will form on the surface of the sponge as well as some cracks, which will create a minimal amount of collapsing). A sponge is usually used in sweet doughs with higher fat contents. It will improve the strength of the dough and compensate for any potential weakening of gluten caused by higher amounts of sugar and fat.

BAKER'S RECIPES

These recipes are all designed to do by hand with little to no extra equipment than what you'd find in a well-stocked home kitchen. Of course, the help of a standing mixer and a dough hook attachment will quicken the final breads. Some doughs are better to hand-mix so they don't heat up too much—and besides, building gluten with your own fingers and palms will ultimately make you a better bread maker.

It's easier and more precise to weigh out ingredients with a digital scale. Cup measurements have been included, just in case you don't have a scale, but your measurements will be less precise. However you measure, be sure to read each recipe carefully and set out measured ingredients before you begin. Each recipe begins with a special Yeast at Work tutorial to give you a deeper understanding of yeast and how it works practically in your doughs. From commercial yeast to pre-ferments to sourdough, each will give the dough its own unique flavors and textures.

YEAST STYLES REFERENCE GUIDE

Yeast	Flavor	Aroma
Active Dry Yeast	Overripe stone fruit	Stone fruit, alcohol, acid, citrus
Instant Rapid Rise Yeast	High alcohol volatility, sweet overripe banana	Yeast, alcohol, acetic, clove, banana
Caked Fresh Yeast	Toast, banana bread	Banana, clove, lactic, bubblegum
Wild Yeast	Tropical fruit, acidity, tart citrus	Papaya, mango, guava, citrus, acid

Time	Form	Use
Anywhere from 30 minutes to a couple of hours, depending on amount of yeast	Dry large granules stored in a paper packet or jar	Any quick baked goods or bread
Depending on amount of yeast, 30 minutes to several hours; will ferment faster and be more viable than other quick yeast	Dry small granules stored in a paper packet or jar	Any quick baked goods or bread
Anywhere from an hour to overnight fermentation, depending on how much yeast is used	Slightly wet and compressed in a brick form, wrapped in paper	Breads and pastry
8 to 48 hours, depending on desired acidity and complexity	Slightly wet, stiff dough to liquid, porridgelike; stored in a sealable container or jar	Any bread or pastry that needs a longer fermentation time

YEAST AT WORK:
HOW RIPENED SOURDOUGH STARTER AIDS A SLOW RISE

A commercial or dry yeast varietal can enrich a dough—and when you let the dough rise at cold temperatures overnight, you'll only further highlight bready, yeasty flavor qualities. A small amount of sourdough starter will also support the rapid rise yeast in a longer fermentation. To make a sourdough starter and then ripen it, follow these steps:

1. Combine **100 grams (½ cup) high-protein bread flour** with **50 grams (¼ cup) rye flour** in a small container. Add **150 grams (⅔ cup) filtered water** that's at 68 to 77°F (20 to 25°C). Stir vigorously to aerate.

2. Cover with plastic wrap, and poke holes in the plastic wrap to make sure there is good oxygen flow. Place in a warm place, 75 to 85°F (23.8 to 29.4°C), and let sit 12 to 24 hours.

3. Check for the beginnings of fermentation. You should see multiple bubbles and a clear increase in volume of the original mixture. Remove **14 grams of starter** and feed it with **100 grams (½ cup) high-protein bread flour** and **100 grams (½ cup) filtered water** that's at 68 to 77°F (20 to 25°C). Going forward, feed accordingly for your baking needs.

4. To ripen your starter, take **3 grams (½ teaspoon) of starter** and mix it with **15 grams (1 tablespoon) bread flour** and **15 grams (1 tablespoon) filtered water** that's at 68 to 77°F (20 to 25°C). Cover your mixture and let it sit at room temperature for 12 to 24 hours, depending on how active your starter is. You can use the float test to see if your starter is ready to use.

continued

PLUMP + SOFTIES

Makes 5 small rolls

These lovely, squishy soft rolls can be used for sandwiches or hamburgers. The fragrant fermentation character will pair well with fruit jams and nut butters.

Equipment

Scale (or measuring cups)

Dough scraper

Bench scraper

Half sheet pan or cookie sheet

Parchment paper

Pastry brush

Ingredients

Water

18 grams (1 tablespoon) instant dry rapid rise yeast

2 tablespoons ripened sourdough starter (see Yeast at Work, page 94)

2 whole eggs

1 egg yolk

112 grams (½ cup) white granulated sugar

9 grams (2 teaspoons) salt

56 grams (¼ cup) vegetable or olive oil (not extra-virgin)

566 grams (4½ cups) high-protein bread flour

50 grams (¼ cup) heavy cream (optional)

1. In a bowl, mix 282 grams (1½ cups) water that's at 68 to 77°F (20 to 25°C) with yeast and sourdough starter until dissolved and fully incorporated.

2. In a separate bowl, beat one egg and yolk with a fork, then incorporate into the yeast, along with sugar.

3. Add flour and knead until dough forms into a ball and no dry parts or clumps are left. Add salt and knead until fully incorporated.

4. Slowly pour in oil and knead in increments until oil has fully laminated dough. Cover bowl and let dough rise for 30 minutes.

5. Fold dough and let it rise for another 30 minutes. Fold the dough again and place into the refrigerator overnight or for 10 to 15 hours.

continued

6. Using a dough scraper, turn the dough out onto a lightly floured surface. Using a bench scraper, divide it into 5 (200-gram) long, rectangular pieces. Preheat the oven to 350°F (177°C).

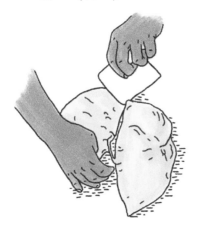

Best Practices: In this recipe, fat is added at the end, after the dough has fully come together. This practice is called *doppio impasto*, which means double or twice dough. It's meant to almost laminate the final dough, which gives these rolls their soft and plump quality. Be careful not to overknead the dough. Just knead enough to incorporate the oil. Overheating this dough may cause the yeast to overproduce alcohol instead of carbon dioxide, resulting in tearing in the final dough structure.

7. Pre-shape the dough into logs: One by one, flatten the rectangular pieces so that the longer edge is parallel to your body. Fold the far horizontal edge toward you, and press the edge to the center of the rectangle. If you have stray pieces, put them in the middle of the rectangle, as not to have a bumpy outside layer on the final dough shape. Continue rolling and pressing until you've formed a tight log. Roll dough with your palms until it reaches the desired length. Cover, and let rest for 30 minutes.

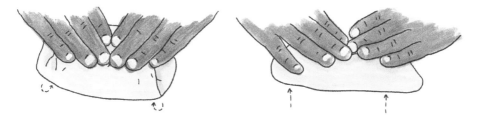

8. Roll the logs into longer strands and twist them into a knot. Place the knots onto a parchment paper–lined sheet pan or cookie tray.

9. In a small cup, beat the remaining egg with 50 grams (¼ cup) of water or heavy cream. Brush egg wash onto the knots and let them rise for 30 minutes or until they double in size.

10. Brush the knots again with egg wash and place into the oven for 20 minutes. Rotate pan and bake for another 10 minutes. Remove from oven and enjoy!

YEAST AT WORK:
THE POOLISH DREAM TEAM

A poolish is a quick ferment using commercial yeast to jump-start fermentation. Instead of waiting weeks for a sourdough starter to properly mature, a poolish can be used to add extensibility, depth of flavor, and shelf life to a bread recipe. A poolish is usually made up of one part flour and one part water with a pinch of yeast. To make poolish, follow these steps:

1. Mix **375 grams (1¾ cup) high-protein bread flour** with **375 grams (1¾ cup) water** that's at 68 to 77°F (20 to 25°C).

2. Add a **small pinch of commercial yeast** and mix in a sealable container.

3. Let this mixture sit overnight or up to 24 hours.

FRENCHIES

Makes 7 demi baguettes

These poolish baguettes are soft on the inside and crunchy on the outside. The malty fermentation flavors pair well with complex or stinky cheese, such as Emmental, Brie, or blue cheese. The long-fermented sandwich bread is perfect for a summer picnic deli sandwich or to dip into hot soup on a cold day.

Equipment

Medium-sized sealable container or plastic wrap

Scale (or measuring cups)

Dough scraper

Bench scraper

Long linen cloth

Wooden bread board (optional)

Half sheet pan or cookie sheet

Parchment paper

Razor blades, sharp knife, or kitchen scissors

Spray bottle filled with ice water

Ingredients

Water

2 grams (½ teaspoon) instant dry rapid rise yeast

46 grams (¼ cup) ripe sourdough starter (see Yeast at Work, page 94)

750 grams (3¾ cups) poolish (see Yeast at Work, page 100)

422 grams (2⅓ cups) high-protein bread flour

2 grams (½ teaspoon) pilsner malt, ground into a flourlike consistency

14 grams (1 tablespoon) salt

continued

1. Pour 170 grams (1 cup) water that's at 68 to 77°F (20 to 25°C), instant dry rapid rise yeast, starter, and poolish into a large tub or mixing bowl. Add the flour and the pilsner malt into the mixture. Mix the ingredients in the bowl until they come together. Cover the bowl or tub and let rise for 20 minutes.

2. Add the salt and knead the dough until the salt is totally incorporated. Let the dough rise for 1 hour, and then do a fold. Let rest for 1 hour.

3. Using a dough scraper, turn the dough out onto a lightly floured surface. Using a bench scraper, divide the dough into 200-gram pieces. Pre-shape the dough into logs (see step 7, page 99). Cover the logs and let them rest for 30 minutes.

4. Shape the logs again into tighter logs or small sandwich-style baguettes. Set up a linen cloth onto a half sheet pan or bread board. Place each baguette in the folds of the cloth. Let these baguettes rise for 20 minutes.

5. Place the baguettes in the refrigerator for 1 to 2 hours or until they are cold to the touch. Meanwhile, preheat your oven to 470°F (243°C).

6. Place each baguette on a half sheet pan or cookie sheet lined with parchment paper. Make three slashes into each baguette using the razor blade. Using the spray bottle, spray cold water on top of each baguette, making sure to coat the entire surface.

7. Bake the baguettes for 15 minutes, rotate the sheet pan, and bake for another 5 minutes or until the baguettes are golden brown. Remove from oven and enjoy!

Best Practices: It's crucial to cover the dough with plastic wrap or in a sealable container. Wrap and cover very well when rising and in between pre-shaping and final shaping of the dough. This dough tends to dry out quickly and form a skin on any exposed areas. To keep the dough soft and malleable, be diligent with this in every step.

YEAST AT WORK:
HOW BEER CAN FEED BREAD

The following recipe has the same grain bill as the rustic witbier in the previous chapter—and it also uses the actual beer in dough, showing how interconnected yeast fermentation in beer and bread is. The recipe will highlight the reasons behind proper nutrient richness using varying yeast subspecies. In fact, pilsner malt and fresh beer come packed with nutrient-rich sugar. To test the total conversion from starch to sugar in the beer, use the iodine test.

1. Take **50 grams (¼ cup) beer** and place it into a small bowl.

2. Using a small dropper, add **2 drops iodine** to the beer.

3. Swirl it around. If the drops remain black, starch hasn't sufficiently converted to sugar. If it dissolves into a clear solution, you're golden.

SOURDOUGH BEER BREAD

Makes 3 boules

The rustic wit bread is fragrant and malty with the slight spice of rye. The crumb is chewy, while the crust is dark and crusty. This bread tastes like a fresh New York bagel and pairs well with salty fish and cream cheese. A perfect accompaniment to Sunday brunch or matched with a dinner of cedar plank smoked fish.

Equipment

Scale (or cups)

Dough scraper

Bench scraper

Plastic wrap

Bread basket for rising

Dutch oven with lid, cast-iron or enamel

Razor blades, sharp knife, or kitchen scissors

Ingredients

Water

300 grams (1½ cups) rustic wit (see page 72)

250 grams (1¼ cups) ripe sourdough starter (see Best Practices, page 107)

1500 grams (7½ cups) high-protein bread flour

200 grams (1 cup) dark whole-grain rye flour

15 grams (1 tablespoon) pilsner malt, ground into a flourlike consistency

30 grams (2½ tablespoons) salt

Rice flour for dusting

continued

1. Pour 860 grams (4¾ cups) water that's at 68 to 77°F (20 to 25°C) into a large mixing bowl or tub. Pour the beer into the water. Place starter into the water and mix it around until it is fully incorporated and bubbles are noticeable on the surface.

2. Add the flours and pilsner malt.

3. Mix until dough comes together and there are no lumps. Cover the dough and let it rest for 30 minutes.

4. Add the salt into the dough and knead it until the salt is fully incorporated into the dough.

5. Cover the dough and let it rise for 2 hours. Do a fold and let rise for 1 hour. Do a second fold and then let it rise for 1 more hour.

6. After the bulk fermentation, turn the dough out onto a lightly floured surface. Scrape out the bowl or tub using the dough scraper. Using the bench knife and scale, divide the dough and weigh it out into 1000-gram pieces.

7. Roll these pieces into rounds, and let them rest for 30 minutes under plastic wrap.

8. Shape the relaxed dough into a round or the shape of your bread basket. Lightly dust your bread basket with rice flour and place the dough inside. Let the dough rise for 30 minutes and place it into the refrigerator for 8 to 15 hours.

9. When you are ready to bake, preheat the Dutch oven inside a 500°F (260°C) oven. Place the dough in the Dutch oven. Score the dough using a razor blade. Place the cover on the Dutch oven, immediately lower the temperature to 450°F (232°C), and bake for 40 minutes.

10. Remove the lid and bake another 5 to 10 minutes. Remove from oven and enjoy!

Best Practices: Make sure 12 to 24 hours before starting this recipe to feed your starter accordingly: Take **75 grams (⅓ cup) sourdough starter** and mix it with **250 grams (1¼ cups) water** that's at 68 to 77°F (20 to 25°C). Mix **250 grams (1¼ cups) flour** and mix in the starter water mixture. Let this mixture sit for 12 to 24 hours or until your starter is ripe. Now you can start this recipe.

YEAST AT WORK:
LIGHT LEAVENING WITH OLDER STARTER

What to do with the leftover starter is a question that every baker asks themselves at some point. Every time a starter is fed, 80% of it is "unusable" and most of the time thrown away. Whereas a ripe starter will impart fruity flavors and aromas, an overripe starter will impart a buttery, cheesy flavor known as diacetyl. An overripe leftover starter will also lose some of its viability and rising power. For bread, this can be problematic, but for crackers it is the perfect fit. To use starter for crackers, follow these steps:

1. When separating your starter during feeding time, take 80% and place it in a sealable reusable container.

2. This can be stored in the refrigerator until it is ready to be used.

3. When you have enough starter to make crackers, follow the recipe for Sourdough Crackers on the next page.

SOURDOUGH CRACKERS

Makes 1 sheet pan of crackers

These amazing vegan crackers are slightly tart and deliciously cheesy—the perfect balance of crispy and chewy. Surprisingly addictive and ready to be dipped into hummus or guacamole, they're a great snack for long car trips or to spread out generously next to a charcuterie board. For an extra treat, try adding 100 grams of crushed nuts or seeds into the cracker dough. Or toss the finished crackers in garlic powder, onion powder, and dill for a delicious ranch flavor.

Equipment

Scale (or cups)

Dough scraper

Bench scraper

Half sheet pan or cookie sheet

Parchment paper

Pastry brush

Pizza cutter

Ingredients

Water

300 grams (1½ cups) leftover sourdough starter

200 grams (1 cup) whole-grain wheat flour

350 grams (1¾ cups) high-protein bread flour

Olive oil spray

5 grams (1 teaspoon) salt

1. In a large bowl, mix 100 grams (½ cup) water that's at 68 to 77°F (20 to 25°C) and sourdough starter. Add in whole-grain wheat flour, and mix until the flour is incorporated and there are no lumps. Add in the high-protein bread flour 100 grams (½ cup) at a time, until the dough comes together and forms a ball.

continued

2. Using the dough scraper, turn it out onto a flat surface. Add the salt into the dough by placing the salt on the table and kneading the dough onto the salt. Keep kneading and incorporating flour into the dough until the dough is very stiff. Wrap it tightly in plastic wrap and place it in the refrigerator for 3 days to increase perceived acidity in the final crackers.

3. Place the dough on a well-floured surface and roll it out into a large rectangle.

4. When you're ready to bake, preheat the oven to 350°F (176.6°C). Transfer the dough onto a parchment paper–lined cookie sheet or half sheet pan. Spray the top of the dough with olive oil spray (or lightly brush it with your desired oil or fat). Using a pizza cutter, cut the rectangle into small cracker squares.

5. Sprinkle salt to taste on top of the crackers and place them in the oven for 15 to 20 minutes, rotating pan after the first 10 minutes.

6. When the crackers are golden brown and some are puffed up, they are ready. Cool and enjoy!

Best Practices: This dough must be quite stiff yet still pliable. After 3 days fermenting in the fridge, it will become wetter and more relaxed. If the original dough isn't stiff enough, it will be difficult to roll out. Try adding the flour slowly by placing it on a flat work surface and kneading the dough onto the flour until it is totally incorporated. If the final dough is still too soft and slack to roll out, more flour can be added right before rolling out.

RECIPES

CHAPTER 6

YEAST EXPERIMENTS

You're standing on a hill, looking down into a valley with a quick babbling brook. The sun beats down on you as a cool mellow breeze passes by, making the hairs on your arm stick up. All around are fruit trees with blossoming flowers and bees buzzing from here to there. It's beautiful, especially when you look closer: There's a white powder coating the fruit's skins—even the dandelions at your feet have a film of gray dust. It's not dirt—it's a collection of living microbes.

Yeast cling to the hairs on your arms and travel in the wind. They are everywhere.

The ability to take the seemingly hidden and use it to make a loaf of bread or a batch of beer is extraordinary when you think about it, as if nature and science are working side by side for your benefit. It's why delving into bread and beer yeast fermentation can be so interesting and fun.

By now, you may want to go even deeper. You already have a better grasp on the concepts and insights that will lend a hand when brewing and baking at home. What's next? It's time to create your own cultures and recipes, and experiment on your own.

The following projects are meant to make brewing and baking unique to you by helping you master yeast techniques, ultimately allowing you to create something special and personal. These experiments will let you peer further into the world of yeast, so keep your eyes open to all the possibilities around you, grabbing yeast and seeing fermentation in everything. From your own body to the outdoors to the beer in your refrigerator, yeast is there waiting. Can you catch it?

CULTIVATING YEAST FROM STORE-BOUGHT BREWS

Makes 1 liter starter

A lot of commercial beers are force carbonated. That is, as the beer moves from the tank to the bottling line, carbon dioxide is pushed through a carbonation stone.

Traditionally, carbonation was added to a cask or a bottle by way of bottle conditioning. Conditioning in the bottle is done by adding priming sugar during the packaging process, where it meets with the beer, which has some suspended yeast left over from the fermentation. Once in the bottle with priming sugar, the yeast referment and carbonate the beer. It's very similar to the champagne method in wine making.

Craft brewers have classically taken the extra care and time to bottle condition their beers. For example, Belgian beers are commonly bottle conditioned and aged in the bottle. In select American craft beers or European wild ales, you can see the yeast cake used for bottle conditioning at the bottom of the bottle. This yeast is awaiting your attention. Maybe you are just curious enough to cultivate it and use it in your own brew.

Have you ever tasted a beer and wished you could harness those flavors and aromas in your own home brew? Since every brewer has their own unique house flavor and specific yeast can be applied to specific beers, you can now enjoy recreating that beer and making it your own. Caution: Not all breweries condition their beer with the same yeast that was used to ferment the beer. Some use special bottling yeast derived from wine yeast to produce a neutral flavor and guarantee a more precise bottle conditioning. Brewers who are interested in keeping tradition of a more rustic

continued

and authentic wild ale, however, will use the same yeast for fermentation and bottle conditioning. The resulting beer will not be consistent or dependable, but it will be special with deep complexities.

How do you know that your favorite beer still has the yeast a beer maker fermented that delectable beverage with? Well, you never know until you try it, though many say so on the label. There are also rumors online about which beer bottles you can or cannot harvest yeast from, but the best way to be sure is to brew a batch and see for yourself. It's easier than you think to harvest yeast from your favorite bottle of beer to make your own culture. Note that you will need a small flame torch, which you can find at hardware stores.

Equipment

3-gallon pot

Spatula

2-quart (2-liter) mason jar

5-quart (5-liter) mason jar

Isopropyl alcohol spray bottle

Flame torch

Ingredients

200 grams (7 oz) plain dried malt extract (DME)

1 teaspoon yeast nutrient

2 quarts (2 liters) water

Your favorite bottle of bottle-conditioned beer

1. Make a starter wort in a large pot using half of the plain dried malt extract, yeast nutrient, and water in a large pot. Bring the starter mixture to a boil for 20 minutes to sterilize it.

2. Pour the starter mixture into a sanitized mason jar and place it in the refrigerator until it reaches 70°F (21°C).

3. Decant the beer, preferably into a pint glass so you can enjoy it later. Be careful not to disturb the yeast dregs at the bottom of the beer. Swirl the bottom dregs from the bottle and pitch them into a mason jar. Cover the jar, but do not tighten the lid. Swirl it periodically and incubate it at room temperature for up to 36 hours.

4. Repeat Step 1, adding the remaining malt extract, yeast nutrient, and water to a 5-quart mason jar and pitching the contents of the 2-quart mason jar to it. Swirl the yeast. Cover the jar, but do not tighten the lid. Swirl it periodically and incubate it up to 36 hours.

5. Store in the refrigerator overnight.

6. Decant the liquor without disturbing the yeast bed. Then decant the yeast from the bottom by swirling it into suspension and placing the yeast back into a sanitized 2-quart mason jar. Store the jar for up to a month in the refrigerator.

ALL HANDS-ON SOURDOUGH STARTERS

Makes 1 or more starters

Why is it that some sourdough starters are incredibly active, while others take many feedings to gain any traction? Why do some sourdough breads need a shorter fermentation (and still yield a wide-open crumb), while the same recipe made by someone else will need a longer fermentation time and still have a dense crumb?

You may have noticed that the temperature of the room, water, and flour can affect how active your starter is, but did you know that the temperature of your hands have even more to do with a starter's viability? Some people are naturally warmer or cooler than others: If you run warm, yeast fermentation is where you belong. You have the power in your hands to speed up fermentation when your surrounding environment is cold.

Hands are also covered in microbes—even after washing—that can affect a starter. These microorganisms live on your hands, which is why people who consistently ferment often become the perfect habitat for those microbes to move from one place to another. So the more those people ferment, the more their ferments, well, ferment. Meanwhile, those who constantly use hand sanitizer, antibacterial soap, or commercial cigarettes filled with formaldehyde and other toxic chemicals can slow or even kill a yeast culture by just touching it. The following project will bring to light how body chemistry, temperature, and environmental factors have an effect on a sourdough starter.

Equipment

Small sealable containers

Sharpie or water-proof marker

Your hands

Your friends' hands

Ingredients

25 grams (2 tablespoons) sourdough starter (see Yeast at Work, page 94)

Water

400 grams (2 cups) flour

1. In a sealable container, mix the sourdough starter with 400 grams (2 cups) water that's at 68 to 77°F (20 to 25°C) using clean hands. With a marker, draw a line on the container to mark where the mixture comes to in the container. Let rise for 6 hours.

2. Draw a new line to mark how much the mixture has risen. Let proof again for 12 hours.

3. Draw a new line to mark how much the mixture has risen. Let proof again for 24 hours. Draw a new line to mark how much the mixture has risen or deflated.

4. Do this project several more times—each with different hand variables. For one experiment, place your hands in ice water for about 30 seconds before mixing the ingredients. For another, wash hands in very warm water. Invite a coworker who smokes cigarettes, your kids, partner, and friends. Have each of them complete this project. Then do it again yourself if you find you're fermenting foods on a regular basis.

5. Then do an analysis: Look at all the sealable containers. Which was the most vigorous and viable? How many hours did it take the starter to mature and then recede? Was your smoker friend's starter viable? Consider it food for thought.

KVASS-INSPIRED BEER

Makes 3 gallons

Kvass is a fizzy drink that some call Russian cola. For centuries people would drink it because most water sources were tainted. For those with less means, it was a good source of B vitamins, calories, and nutrition. Similar to kombucha, kvass is low in alcohol but relies on lactic acid for alcohol production instead of acidic acid. Traditionally, it's made with bread, which technically makes it a hard soda instead of a beer. But in the following recipe, you'll add rye malt to further bring up the alcohol content and transform this classic bread beverage into an actual beer!

Classic kvass is usually overly sweet because it uses molasses to mimic the flavor of soda. A truly delicious alternative is to treat kvass in a similar way to a kettle sour. Think slightly tart with a jammy quality from the added fruit yet light and crisp, crushable, and finishing dry.

Here, you'll use leftover bread and sourdough starter, naturally full of wild yeast and bacteria. Having a high pitch rate of ripe sourdough starter culture will take this recipe to the next level, thanks to a viable culture that promotes the quality and vigor of fermentation. So will ripening the sourdough starter, allowing Saccharomyces and Lactobacillus to be abundant. Bacteria such as Acetobacter and Enterobacter will not be able to compete in the kvass brew with a large pitch rate and an accelerated vigorous fermentation, keeping unwanted microorganisms from spoiling the brew.

Equipment	Ingredients
Large Pot	Water
Spatula	2 lb table sugar (or liquid malt)
Netted laundry bag	6 lb of sourdough bread
5-gallon fermentation vessel	400 grams (2 cups) rye malt
Airlock	6 lb macerated local fruit (such as cherries, apricots, or guava and passionfruit)
	2 quarts of sourdough starter, ripened 24 hours (see Yeast at Work, page 94)

1. In a large pot, heat 3 gallons water to 180°F (83°C). Add the table sugar and mix with a spatula.

2. Quarter the bread, making sure the pieces are small enough for an even distribution of the water but large enough that they don't instantly turn into mush. Place bread in a netted laundry bag and steep in the hot water for 3 hours.

3. Add the rye malt to the pot, and let the water cool to 104°F (40°C).

4. Move the sourdough bread and water mixture into a pre-sanitized 5-gallon fermentation vessel. Add macerated fruit.

5. Pitch the ripened sourdough starter into the vessel. Secure the lid with an airlock and allow it to sit for a month.

6. Rack off the mixture into a 3-gallon container for bottling or kegging, and enjoy!

DRYING OUT STARTERS

Makes 100 grams dried starter

The ability to take liquid active cultures and dry them out is a great resource. This is not a new idea. There's a whole industry around making active dry yeast by drying liquid culture into thousands of granular pieces. Though for someone who keeps a sourdough starter at home, this technique can seem foreign and strange. But in fact it can ease the worry of neglecting a sourdough starter or even killing it by having a backup stash of the dried stuff.

Besides, nurturing a sourdough starter can take over your life. Especially if you're not baking bread every day, it's helpful to have a good plan for storing it while keeping it healthy and viable. Thus, drying your sourdough starter to thrust the yeast into a latent state, in which they'll store all their energy in the form of glycogen and await the day they're reactivated by you and can multiply once again makes perfect sense.

Norwegian farmhouse yeasts have been dried for decades. Kveik, yeast in Norway, was stored on oak rings that were soaked in the yeast matter after a fermentation and then set to dry over a fireplace in the barn. These yeast are renowned for easy hydrating and dehydrating, which makes these cultures especially easy to use. Just don't go placing a random sourdough starter over a hot fire to dry it—it won't work. (Though you will find the proper method in the next section.) Kveik yeast is special in that it can withstand high heat because it's a hybrid of more modern English yeast and ancient Asian yeast, which have genes to protect them from high-temperature environments. It's a similar mechanism found in thermophilic bacteria living in volcanoes.

Drying out a sourdough starter is also a good choice when refrigerator space is minimal. Instead of needing a medium to large jar to hold an active or hibernating starter, a dried starter can be stored in a small plastic bag—perfect for traveling or sharing with loved ones. Being able to bring your starter with you when visiting family and friends will let you bake for them anywhere in the world. Next you will find the steps necessary not only to dry your sourdough starter but to rehydrate it as well.

Equipment Needed

Flat sheet pan or cookie sheet

Flexible dough scraper or spatula

Parchment paper

Resealable plastic bag

Ingredients for Drying

100 grams (½ cup) or more sourdough starter (see Yeast at Work, page 94)

Ingredients for Rehydrating Day 1

5 grams (1 teaspoon) dried sourdough starter

15 grams (1 tablespoon) water

15 grams (1 tablespoon) flour

Ingredients for Rehydrating Day 2

7 grams (½ tablespoon) water

15 grams (1 tablespoon) flour

Ingredients for Rehydrating Day 3

5 grams (1 teaspoon) water

5 grams (1 teaspoon) flour

continued

1. To dry a starter, use a dough scraper to spread sourdough starter onto a parchment paper–lined sheet pan. Make sure the starter is spread evenly and thinly. (If the starter is too thick, it will not dry fast enough, and harmful bacteria may attack it.) Leave the starter in a cool dry place for 1 hour or until it is entirely dry.

2. Once the starter is dry, it should peel easily from the parchment paper. Place the shards of starter in a jar or use a mortar and pestle to break them up and place in a sealable plastic bag. The starter can now be stored in a cool dry cabinet or in the freezer.

3. Rehydrating your sourdough starter is a 3-day process. On day 1, take your dried starter and dissolve it in room-temperature water. Add flour and mix gently. Leave in a sealable container overnight.

4. On day 2, add water and flour. Mix and leave in a sealable container overnight.

5. On day 3, add water and flour to the mixture. You should start seeing activity at this point: small bubbles and a sweet fermentation aroma. If you don't see anything at this point, repeat the steps until fermentation is detected.

6. Continue feeding your starter according to your bread-baking needs.

WILD YEAST HONEY CAPTURE

Makes 1 liter starter

Wild capture can be done a few different ways. As discussed in the previous chapters, yeast love to dwell on the skins of fruit where sugar is plentiful. Yeast is also on our skin, on plant life, and in the air. Where your yeast culture's origins are will determine the flavors and aromas that the yeast impart, as well as how active the culture can become.

Yeast is also found on bees—probably because of all their contact with fresh pollen, fragrant flowers, and sweet honey. Raw honey will actually have parts of bees in it and therefore a plentiful amount of yeast! In this project, you will be cultivating yeast from raw honey to make a bread or a beer starter that will impart complex flavors into beer and bread. Once you've tried this technique with honey, look around and see where else you may want to find a wild culture: The sky's the limit.

Collecting wild yeast samples from honey is easier than you may think. The things to focus on when collecting this sample are aeration and amino acids. Honey doesn't have enough amino acids to get natural yeast going on its own. This is where the use of yeast nutrient comes into play. Yeast nutrient will add free amino acids and essential vitamins to your culture, ensuring that the wild yeast will have what it needs to thrive. Aeration is important because the wild new yeast need oxygen to form sterols to strengthen their cell walls. Keeping all of this in mind while doing your wild capture will assure a successful outcome.

Equipment	Ingredients
3-gallon pot	400 grams (2 cups) raw honey
Spatula	200 grams (1 cup) low-gravity (1.010 to 1.020) unhopped starter wort (see page 117)
1-quart mason jar	
Isopropyl alcohol spray bottle	

1. Put the raw honey in a sanitized 1-quart mason jar. Add starter wort into the mason jar—just enough to dissolve the honey. Leave enough room for fermentation activity at the top.

2. Wrap the seal between the lid and jar with plastic wrap. Shake vigorously to aerate, and then leave it in a dark, room-temperature place.

3. Within a few days you should see signs of fermentation taking place. A yeast sediment will eventually form at the bottom of the jar. When swirling the jar, you should see carbon dioxide leaving the solution.

4. You can now plate the yeast (see Strain Isolation, page 128).

5. Next, try using orange blossom honey and compare it to using honey from the thistle flower. Depending on the honey, the culture will change in the flavor and aroma profiles it puts forth.

STRAIN ISOLATION

Makes 2 liters yeast

You now have your unique wild honey yeast culture (see Wild Yeast Honey Capture, page 126). The first thing you may want to do is brew with it. But before you start your first wild honey home brew, it's key to know which yeast will give you the best result.

A mixed wild culture fermentation is as close as you will ever get to replicating ancient fermentation practices. But the culture you cultivated may be questionable with an array of bacteria hitching a ride with the yeast. So you'll want to select the proper colonies and separate the dubious from the desired. You'll also want to know what makes each strain unique and what beer styles and ingredients they work best with. This will give a brewer the control needed to continuously use yeast reliably. Getting to know your yeast culture is easier than you think. The following projects will teach you how to plate, streak, and isolate the yeast you so desire.

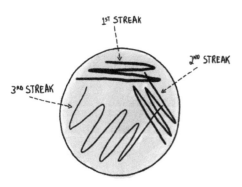

To do this, it's probably best to isolate those wild yeast colonies and create agar plates. Agar plates are made by using agar as a solid growth medium in a petri dish with other growth nutrients and are used to culture microorganisms. You'll make a plate and then simply streak the culture onto the agar plate to isolate the microbes. After some time, depending on microbe population and incubation temperature, they will multiply and grow. Some of these colonies will be readily visible to the naked eye. At this point you want to select the colony you like and grow it up in higher volumes.

To increase the odds of isolating a pure culture, select one colony to propagate. It's ideal to select at least a few colonies to increase the genetic diversity of your culture, but without the benefit of a microscope, you won't know if the colonies you've selected are the same. So you'll streak another plate using the same growing culture to get the best isolation. In the end, you'll have a lot of pure cultures with good genetic diversity.

Sanitation and cleanliness are paramount in protecting an isolated culture from contamination. Take extra care to make sure everything is wiped down with isopropyl alcohol and that all equipment has been sanitized with either alcohol or fire. Since you're not working in a clean lab with a hood, you're more likely to get contaminated plates. So use a small flame torch (found in hardware stores) on the workbench you're plating to prevent common contaminants.

Equipment	Ingredients
Small pot	1 tablespoon agar-agar
Thermometer	1 tablespoon dry malt extract (DME)
At least 5 petri dishes and lids	.75 grams (¼ teaspoon) yeast nutrient
Plastic wrap	Water
Resealable plastic bag	1 cup wort
Small flame torch	Wild Yeast Honey Capture (see page 126)
70% isopropyl alcohol	2 liters of starter wort (see page 117)
Paper clip	

continued

1. In order to create an agar plate, create a wort by heating agar-agar and dry malt extract, yeast nutrient, and 1 cup water in a small pot until it is near boiling. Then stir in the agar. Bring the mixture to a boil. Agar and wort won't successfully bind otherwise.

2. Let the mixture cool 5 to 10 minutes until the temperature is 104°F (40°C). Watch your pot closely, since agar sets quickly and still needs to be a thick liquid when decanted into the dish.

3. Pour a small layer of liquid onto the petri dish and move to an area with little wind disruption. Let the liquid cool before covering it with the lid to prevent condensation from forming. This will reduce the likelihood of mold growth. Mold will grow, but that shouldn't deter you. You can still isolate wild yeasts from around the mold.

4. If a good agar-to-wort ratio was used, the agar plates should set within a few minutes. If you find your plates aren't setting, you may need to reboil your mixture with more agar added.

5. Wrap the edges of the plate lid with stretchable plastic wrap to protect from contaminants and prevent the plate from drying out. Store the plates upside down in a warm, dark place to incubate for a few days. (You can later store them upside down in a resealable plastic bag in the refrigerator for future use.)

6. When you're ready to use the plate, create an updraft with a turned-on blowtorch standing on a workbench or counter to keep your work area free of unwanted microbes.

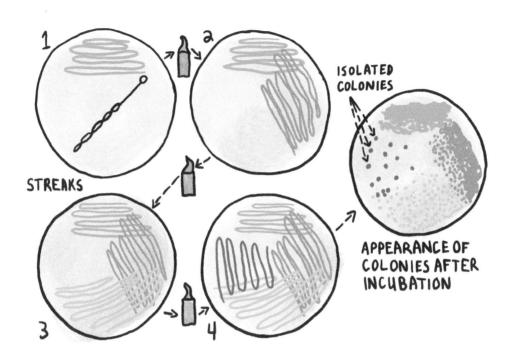

STREAKS

ISOLATED COLONIES

APPEARANCE OF COLONIES AFTER INCUBATION

7. Remove the lid from the upside-down agar plate and decant the condensate. Place plate back on top of the lid, upside down, remembering not to drip condensate on the agar.

8. Sterilize paper clip by placing it under the torch flame until it glows. Let it cool for 30 seconds.

9. Shake mason jar of wild honey capture. Dip the paper clip into your liquid culture to collect a small amount.

continued

10. Remove the lid from the agar plate. Place the droplet of the liquid from the paper clip onto the agar medium at the outermost edge. Gently move the liquid around at an angle in the corner of the plate.

11. Sterilize the paper clip under the flame again. Streak a zigzag of lines in the corner of the plate adjacent to the original inoculation site.

12. Sterilize the paper clip again. Go back to the previous streaks and drag the paper clip across them, creating lines in another direction. Continue repeating this process until you've streaked in four different directions on the edge of the plate. Do not streak into already zigzagged space, as you don't want to collect any biological debris that you have already streaked out.

13. Flip the plate upside down and place it on top of the lid. Incubate in a dark warm area for several days or up to several weeks, monitoring along the way to make sure just 30% of the plate is covered with growing yeast and mold.

14. When it's ready, retrieve your streaked plate from storage. It should be a cornucopia of microbes. Select a colony that shows medium-size, white to off-white, nicely round, individual colonies.

15. Sterilize the paper clip under your burner. Let it cool before dipping it into the chosen colony to collect a sample. Streak a fresh plate and let it incubate. Continue picking single colonies, restreaking, and incubating plates until you have one where all the colonies growing have the same shape, size, and color.

16. Once you're satisfied that you have a uniform plate of organisms, select one colony from the plate using a sterilized paper clip. Dunk it into a small 100-ml jar of the boiled wort. Seal and shake vigorously.

17. In order to create a starter, repeat the process and step up the ingredient list by about 10 times until you've built up to a pitchable quantity—from 100ml to 1000ml to 2000ml. Now it's ready to test in your next batch of home brew.

GLOSSARY

Aerate: To expose to the action or effect of air or to cause air to circulate through.

Biofuel: A fuel derived directly from living matter.

Bottle Dregs: The yeast sediment at the bottom of a sour beer that contains the microbes responsible for transforming wort into beer.

CBD: Cannabidiol, the second most active ingredient of cannabis.

Chitin: A fibrous substance consisting of polysaccharides and forming the major constituent in the exoskeleton of arthropods and the cell walls of fungi.

Diastatic: Refers to the diastatic enzymes that are created as the grain sprouts. These convert starches to sugars, which yeast eat.

Eukaryote: An organism consisting of one or more cells, where the genetic material is DNA in the form of chromosomes contained within a distinct nucleus.

Germination: The process by which an organism grows from a seed or similar structure. The most common example of germination is the sprouting of a seedling from a seed of an angiosperm or gymnosperm.

Hydrocarbon: A compound of hydrogen and carbon, such as any of those which are the chief components of petroleum and natural gas.

Hydrolysis: The chemical breakdown of a compound owing to reaction with water.

Hyphae: Each of the branching filaments that make up the mycelium of a fungus.

Progeny: A descendant or the descendants of a person, animal, or plant; offspring.

Propagate: To breed specimens of (a plant or animal) by natural processes from the parent stock.

Respiration: A process in living organisms involving the production of energy, typically with the intake of oxygen and the release of carbon dioxide from the oxidation of complex organic substances.

Sanitation: Conditions relating to public health, especially the provision of clean drinking water and adequate sewage disposal.

Sterilize: To clear an object of bacteria or other living microorganisms.

THC: Tetrahydrocannabinol, a crystalline compound that's the main active ingredient of cannabis.

INGREDIENT + EQUIPMENT RESOURCES

Flour: Central Milling (www.kgbakerysupply.com) and King Arthur Flour (www.kingarthurflour.com)

Hops and Malt: More Beer! (www.morebeer.com)

Salt: SaltWorks (www.seasalt.com)

Yeast and Lactic Acid Pitch: Bootleg Biology (bootlegbiology.com), White Labs (www.whitelabs.com), and Real Brewers Yeast (www.realbrewersyeast.com)

Digital Scales: Taylor USA (www.taylorusa.com)

Dough Scraper and Bench Knife: Rackmaster (www.rackmaster.com)

Bread Boards: TMB Baking Equipment (www.tmbbaking.com)

Proofing Baskets: TMB Baking Equipment (www.tmbbaking.com)

Cast-Iron Dutch Oven: Lodge (www.lodgemfg.com)

The Challenger Bread Pan: Challenger Breadware (www.challengerbreadware.com)

Basic Home-Brewing Equipment: Home Brew Supply (www.homebrewsupply.com)

Sous Vide Wand: Anova Culinary (www.anovaculinary.com) and Joule by ChefSteps (www.chefsteps.com)

FURTHER READING

Bread by Jeffrey Hamelman

Jeffrey Hamelman is one of the few Certified Master Bakers in the United States. He has taught in baking and pastry schools around the world. He is the foremost expert in everything sourdough. His book, *Bread*, has all the basics about the wonderful subject—plus some amazing recipes.

Advanced Bread and Pastry by Michel Suas

This book is a professional's approach to bread and pastry. It has all the techniques you need as a professional baker. This guide is required for pastry to bread students everywhere to study diligently and commit to memory.

How to Brew by John Palmer

John Palmer literally wrote the book on how to brew. Considered the bible of home brewing, this work by Palmer is one of the more technical pieces of literature for brewing on the market. Everything you need to know for beginners and advanced brewers alike. A real gem.

The Oxford Companion to Beer by Garrett Oliver

An encyclopedia of beer that's rich with the history and complexities of all the world beer styles. Garrett Oliver, the brewmaster of Brooklyn Brewery, delivers the most comprehensive book on the world's beers—from craft beer to imports to domestics. Check it out.

Microbe Hunters by Paul de Kruif

This book tells the story of all the great microbe hunters from Antonie van Leeuwenhoek to Paul Ehrlich. Stories for children and adults alike, it is a fantastical and technical view into the history of microorganisms and those who were curious enough to find them.

INDEX

ABOUT THE AUTHOR

Harmony Sage is the co-owner and cofounder of Long Beach Beer Lab, Long Beach Bread Lab, and Long Beach Spirits Lab in Southern California. She is a classically trained pastry chef who grew up in the kitchen with her parents and grandparents and later worked at the Ritz Carlton under James Satterwhite. Home brewing with her husband, Levi Fried, in Israel later led her to take her natural interests and talents working with yeast fermentation and turn them into a business. Her life is usually overflowing with fermentation, but when she doesn't have her hands in dough or isn't knee-deep in malted barley, she's hanging out with her two teenage boys, Dov and Eitan; swimming in the ocean; or cycling along the Pacific Coast Highway.